ILENE BEATTY

ARAB AND JEW IN THE LAND OF CANAAN

Chicago • 1957

HENRY REGNERY COMPANY

Manufactured in the United States of America. Library of Congress Catalogue Card Number 57-10264.

To MY COMPATRIOTS, the American Jews, as exemplified by one of their number, my friend, Miss Josephine Rosenberg. Theirs is a difficult situation. Theirs is a difficult decision. May they choose in accordance with their American ideals of peace and brotherhood and the precepts of their own ancient prophets.

ACKNOWLEDGMENTS

GRATEFUL ACKNOWLEDGMENT and many thanks are due to the authors, editors and publishers for permission to quote from the following books, magazines and news sources: *The Archaeology of Palestine* by W. F. Albright (Penguin Books, Ltd., Harmondsworth, Middlesex); *Recent Discoveries in Bible Lands* by W. F. Albright (Funk & Wagnalls); *The Biblical Period* by W. F. Albright (The Biblical Colloquium); *World Almanac and Book of Facts,* Harry Hansen, editor, New York *World Telegram and Sun; The Cambridge Ancient History* (Cambridge University Press); *An Encyclopedia of World History* by William Langer (Houghton Mifflin Co.); *What Happened in History* by V. Gordon Childe (Penguin Books, Ltd.); *A Study of History* by Arnold J. Toynbee (Oxford University Press); *The Horse and the Sword,* Vol. VIII, Corridors of Time Series, by Harold Peake and Herbert John Fleure (Yale University Press); *Syrian Pageant* by Wilfrid T. F. Castle (Hutchinson & Co., Ltd.); *Ancient Israel* by Harry M. Orlinsky (Cornell University Press); *Violent Truce* by Commander E. H. Hutchinson (Devin-Adair Co.); *United Nations Report on Palestine,* N. Y., 1947; "Arab vs. Jew" by Wm. Attwood (*Look* magazine); "Tough Little Army" by Don Cook (*Saturday Evening Post*); "Glubb Tells How Our Mid-East Enemies Work" by Sir John Bagot Glubb (*Life* magazine); and news dispatches and items from *Time* magazine, the New York *Times* and the New York *Herald Tribune.*

Hollywood
March 9, 1957

ILENE BEATTY

CONTENTS

ARAB AND JEW

IN THE LAND OF CANAAN

Human Rights

WAR HAS NOT been declared in the Middle East. But it is nonetheless in progress. It can be halted. But peace will not come permanently to that part of the world until the basic cause of the trouble is eradicated. There are many added factors, but in the final analysis, what is the basic cause? It is ISRAEL VS. ARAB.

The American public, suddenly aware of the danger, has come to the point where it wants facts. Any just solution must be based on facts. And an early solution is imperative; otherwise, we on the periphery may find ourselves drawn into another world war.

Anyone can wade through the thousands of pages of United Nations reports on Palestine—but few will. Fortunately there is a more convenient source of information readily accessible to all. It is entirely devoid of emotion, one of the driest and at the same time most reliable in America—*The World Almanac and Book of Facts,* issued yearly, which can be seen in the Reference Room of any public library. The statistics given in this section, taken from *World Almanacs,* 1948-56, are easily found under four headings: Israel, Jordan, Palestine, and the Yearly Chronology of Principal Events.

To set the scene: Throughout history, Palestine has had a long and varied succession of invasions and conquests by outsiders. The present permanent Arab population goes back 1300 years to the Moslem conquest by the followers of the Prophet Mohammed in A.D. 632-638, when those desert Arabs poured into Palestine, settled there, and remained. Turkey took Palestine in 1516/17, and for the following 400 years Palestine's Arab population was under the government of, and was a part of, the Turkish Empire.

In the latter part of the 19th century, the Zionist movement was founded in Middle Europe, and toward the end of the Turkish regime it planted several small Jewish settlements near the Mediterranean coast in Turkish Palstine. Of these, Tel Aviv was to become the most important.

But the Turks had the bad judgment to join with the German Kaiser in World War I. They lost Palestine. The League of Nations Peace Settlement put that small country, 150 miles long and roughly averaging only about 65 miles wide, under a British Mandate to begin September 29, 1923.

The 1946/47 *Yearbook of the United Nations* (page 288) tells us that "The Jews in Palestine in 1914 represented about 6 or 7% of the total population."

But during the British Mandate immigration was stepped up[1], and Tel Aviv grew to a sizable city. At the end of World War II there was world-wide Jewish demand, and especially Jewish-American demand, for partition of Palestine and the creation of an independent Jewish nation.

The general American public, with the horrors of Hitler's concentration camps and gas chambers fresh in its mind, also reacted favorably to the idea. We average Americans knew almost nothing about Palestine's political history during the last 1900 years and could hardly have answered a question on its recent status, whose Mandate it had been under or the name of the government that had preceded the Mandate. But we knew what we had learned in Sunday School—that Palestine had once been the Jewish Promised Land. The Jews now desperately needed a place where they could be safe. Therefore———

President Truman was accused of equal ignorance and accused also of sponsoring the creation of a Jewish state in order to gain the Jewish-American vote in the election of 1948. In fairness to Mr. Truman, his motives were probably as humanitarian as ours, for he is a kindly man; as religious as ours, because he comes from a religious part of the country and was probably brought up on the same Sunday School concepts; and at least as altruistic, for as President he was in a position to know a great deal more about the potential benefits of such a Plan than most of us were. Surely he envisioned not only a haven for the oppressed but a new democratic state that would foster American ideals and, as a small replica of our own nation, set a fine example in the backward Middle East. His intentions—and ours—were good.

American Jews have also been pictured in an unfavorable light and accused of subtle designs in sponsoring Isreal. But they too are Americans, our fellow citizens, and their motives were without doubt even more altruistic than our own and Mr. Truman's, for their cousins (literally, not figuratively) had been the victims of Hitler's gas chambers, and they knew how desperately a haven was needed. We may be sure that every earnest worker raising money for Hadassah, every Jewish-American housewife saving coins in the Israel penny-bank behind the breadbox thought only of providing rehabilitation and medical aid for the skeletal refugees from Europe and the education of their children. Jewish-American men who raised, and gave, millions were equally well intentioned.

Their intentions were good, ours were good, Mr. Truman's were good—all our intentions were good. And certainly the intentions of the United Nations were good.

But the Plan to create a peaceful haven failed completely.

Why? What went wrong?

Perhaps it is that in this list of the well-intentioned, the central characters are missing.

In 1947/48 the UN split Palestine in two, partitioned it. Half was given to the nation now called Israel; and the other half, to the Palestinian Arabs and now a part of the Hashemite Kingdom of Jordan.

Jewish Israel stands on one side of the Partition Line, Arab Jordan on the other. These are the two central characters in the area once called Palestine. Both are autonomous governments, each formulating its own foreign policy.

If the policies of both were actually peaceful, it seems logical that the peace would have been kept.

How can the outside observer determine the real policy of any nation? We cannot judge by words, that we know, for we have heard communist nations shout peace while engaged in bloody aggression.

And we cannot judge by the acts of the private citizens of any nation, for individuals act on their own initiative, according to the way they themselves feel. If we think of our own country, we will realize this. Gangsters and groups organized for purposes of murder operate here in the United States, but such activities do *not* represent US policy. Despite the unending vigilance of Canadian and US Customs officials at their common border, violations are constantly attempted, sometimes with success. But the breaking of customs regulations is certainly *not* the government policy of either the US or Canada. Smugglers of narcotics, and of people, operate across the US-Mexican border, but their activities do *not* represent the policy of either the US or Mexico.

Our conclusion is this: the acts of private persons do not represent government policy in the USA.

And if we are consistent, we must admit that the acts of private Israeli citizens do not represent the policy of the Israel government. And the acts of private Arab citizens do not represent the policy of Arab Palestine, now a part of the Hashemite Kingdom of Jordan.

So it is not the purpose of this book to give a list of the hundreds of Palestinian border incidents involving the *individuals* of either side, for they are *not* indicative of government policy on either side.

In fact their individual activities may be directly opposed to the policy of their government and may serve only to bring blame and condemnation down on that government's head. That particular government may really be trying desperately, with only inadequate police forces, to prevent violation by its own private citizens and thus prevent censure by the United Nations and by world opinion.

So we are not talking about *individuals.*

What then actually reveals a government's intentions and its real program? *Only* the acts of the government.

Only actions taken *on government orders,* by an official department of the government. The army of a nation is an instrument of its government. We may safely say then that the actions of the army of any nation, taken on government orders, represent the policy of that government.

Therefore, in the discussion of Israel vs. Arab, we shall talk about the government policy of each nation as indicated by government (not individual) action.

The actions of each nation will show that nation's good or bad faith, its intent to honor its own signature on the Armistice Agreement to keep the peace; or its intent to violate that agreement. Government action is the criterion.

We shall then trace the resultant course of events which has changed Palestine into what it is today, a slow but foolproof time bomb; and by analysis of our findings, try to discover a solution.

To reach a right solution, a judge reviews the evidence. Shall we do the same?

From the beginning, when the infant Israel was still in a state of gestation awaiting birth, it faced a future prospect of tremendous handicaps. In the territory it hoped to acquire by a partition of Palestine, the unwelcome Jewish residents were far in the minority. If Israel could actually become a nation, it had only the bleak prospect of being outnumbered and outvoted by the majority of citizens who lived in the area.

To overcome this handicap, the Tel Aviv Jews during the years of the British Mandate (1923-48) began what was at first a steady and later a frantic and illegal importation of immigrants for whom they had no room, at last smuggling the wet-backs in and hiding them in warehouses and empty buildings.

When the embryo nation was born on May 15, 1948, it was still almost too weak in numbers to exist. Of the increase in Jewish population at the time of partition, four-fifths (1948 *World Almanac and Book of Facts*, page 534), or approximately 336,000, were immigrants. Many thousands still had to be fed, clothed. Places had to be found for them—houses to live in, farms on which to raise food.

The trouble was that most of the houses and farms were already owned and occupied by Arabs whose forbears had owned and occupied them continuously for hundreds of years.

So the partition of Palestine's 10,429 square miles favored Israel a little by giving it more than half—and that the best half—5,500 square miles of comparatively level, fertile and well-watered farmland along the coast of the Mediterranean (1949 *World Almanac*, page 530).

This left 289 square miles for a projected international Enclave of Jerusalem; and for the Arabs, 4,500 square miles of bare stone mountains known as the Wilderness of Judea, together with the surrounding dry foothill country which was hardly fit for goat grazing.

Partition was preceded and accompanied by violent war between the Arabs and the Israelis. The outraged Arabs refused to give up their own good farmland. The Palestine Conciliation Commission estimated that 80 per cent of land in Israel-occupied territory was owned by Arabs (*UN Document A/1985*, Annex A, page 11, paragraphs 1 and 8).

But the Israelis *had* to have it for their immigrants, and the most effective means of clearing territory was not conventional war between opposing armies, but terrorization of the civilian population. And so, to clear the Arabs out and provide living space for its own newcomers, Israel began a campaign of civilian terrorization against the Arabs living on the Israel side. They ran the Arabs out and took possession of their farms. Then and thereafter they consistently refused either to return the farms or to pay for them.[2]

Israel did not stop there. After its own designated territory was cleared of its Arab inhabitants, Israel went across the Partition Line in efforts to advance its own borders and gain still more land than that already allotted. A classic example of this push-out was the attack across the Line on Deir Yassin, April 9, 1948, more than a month before actual Israel independence.

War had been declared and was being waged tooth and nail by both sides: first in local, spontaneous riots; then by planned attacks with grenades and bombs on trucks, jeeps, bus convoys, armored cars and trains carrying soldiers and ammunition and explosives; then by field engagements.

But the attack on Deir Yassin fell outside the war category, for Deir Yassin was not a military target; it was a civilian village far inside the Arab lines, and the assault followed the expert rules laid down by Hitler in the beginning of World War II, when he drove out millions of civilians who congested the roads of France as they fled. At Deir Yassin the Israelis also advanced with loud speakers blasting. Israeli forces then stormed the Arab village and killed every remaining civilian in sight, including women and children. Two hundred corpses were found by UN investigators (1949 *World Almanac*, page 709).

This massacre, entirely outside the rules of conventional war—and even outside the violent guerrilla practices on both sides, was a crime against society as definite as the murder of one peaceful and innocent individual by another.

By the end of 1948, Israel's campaign of evacuation was so successful that hordes of Arab refugees had fled from their homes on the Israel side of the line and were milling about in utter destitution on the Arab side, waiting for the cessation of hostilities and an armistice which would permit them to return, albeit with some trepidation, to their own homes.

But they never got back. They *never* got back. Despite repeated orders and demands from the UN, Israel simply refused to let them come back.

Instead, the newly-arrived Jewish immigrants were placed in the vacated Arab homes. At last Israel had housing.

But little Israel was a growing boy, and growing boys burst out their seams. How far Israel has burst out will be seen. From here on, the statistics have tongues as eloquent as Caesar's wounds and speak for themselves.

The International Enclave of Jerusalem had never materialized, and Palestine's total area of 10,429 square miles was unwillingly shared between Arabs and Israelis.

Israel's push-out all along the line had been successful.

And continued to be.

Despite the cessation of hostilities, Israel went across the Line on October 21, 1948, (1949 *World Almanac*, page 741) *after* a cease-fire had been agreed, took Beersheba and simply refused to give it up.

Even after the signing of the Armistice, the pushout continued so successfully that the 1950 *World Almanac and Book of Facts* on page 193 reported the area held by Israel as 7,100 square miles. This was a gain for Israel of

1,600 square miles of territory over the amount allotted by the Partition.

By simple subtraction, this reduced the territory remaining for the Arabs to 3,329 *square miles,* less than half the amount held by Israel.

There was a settled Arab population already living in this area of 3,329 square miles. Into this limited space poured the milling throng of Arab refugees, their numbers now mounting into the hundreds of thousands. Destitute, actually hungry, they inundated Arab Palestine in such multitudes as to make anything like adequate feeding and housing an utter impossibility.[3]

Daily they thronged government offices urgently demanding permission to return to their homes. When the UN failed to get Israel's consent to a return, individual Arabs, most of them unarmed, as the reports show,[4] began to cross surreptitiously on their own accord—usually to fetch something they had left behind and needed. "Many Arabs were killed inside Israel trying to retrieve items from their former homes." (Quoted from *Violent Truce* by Commander E. H. Hutchinson, published 1956 by the Devin-Adair Company, New York, N. Y. Copyright 1956 by the Devin-Adair Company. Commander Hutchinson is the former chairman of the Jordan-Israel Mixed Armistice Commission.)

Each of these crossings, no matter how harmless, was technically a violation of the Armistice Agreement and was so reported by the Israeli authorities and so tallied by the UN Armistice Commission to become a black mark against Arab Jordan.

Did these acts represent Jordanian policy? Quite the opposite. The Jordanian government was actually making desperate attempts to stop violations by its own Arabs and with good reason. Jordan was well aware that its own Arab Legion numbered only 20,000 men to Israel's army of 250,000. It behooved the Jordan government to walk a straight path, and it did.[5]

Israel, with its 1,600 square miles of new territory, had a lot of extra space. With the Jewish immigrants already housed in Arab properties in the area originally allotted, Israel had empty miles along its newly advanced borders. Occupants were needed at once to fill and protect this space, lest the dispossessed Arabs creep back to their homes, reoccupy them, and become a source of weakness along the frontier.

And so began a tremendous campaign called the In-Gathering. The Israeli government collected Jews from the ends of the earth and transported them free of charge to Israel, not only to fill up the empty border spaces but to provide voters, civilian work battalions, and manpower for the army.

By April of 1951, Israel had received 559,616 immigrants (1952 *World Almanac*, page 329). They continued to arrive in such numbers that by the end of that year the Jewish population had increased to 1,230,000 (1952 *World Almanac*, page 330).

Israel's area, by means of the continued relentless push-out, had grown by this time to 7,800 square miles, (1952 *World Almanac*, page 329), a further gain of 700 square miles. But its population was expected to reach 2,000,000 by 1953 (1953 *World Almanac*, pages 361-2).

This cutting off of Arab Palestine's body had left it by subtraction a total space of 2,629 square miles for the settled Arab population and the refugees. More Arabs had been dispossessed, and by 1953, *their* number had reached the staggering estimated total of 1,000,000 (*World Almanac* for 1954, page 359).

Israel's first step—the illegal importation of an excessive number of immigrants while under the British Mandate, called for the next—more space for housing the immigrants, then more immigrants to fill up the extra space, then more space for the surplus immigrants.

And the In-Gathering still produced a human flood-tide which rolled into Israel like the smashing billows from the Mediterranean in a winter storm. Room, food, houses had to be found.

A gain of 700 square miles in three years was not enough. A forward-looking program for taking care of these newcomers had to be formulated and put into action. It was.

Covering a two-year period from 1953-55 (the Armistice was supposed to be in effect), the Israeli *government* made a series of systematic attacks on Arab villages. If any pretext was needed, the Arab refugees crossing the line supplied it, and once the sequence was put in motion, a set train of events automatically followed which brought other Israeli attacks in endless succession. This was the way it worked.

After Israel had made the attack and driven the Arabs out of their village, the practice was to set up a new Israeli settlement there, often before the dust of battle settled. If that site continued under UN surveillance, then the settlement was set up on some other nearby spot from which the terrified Arabs had also fled.

But the Arabs who had succeeded in escaping with their lives were usually lurking not far away from the homes they had left. Israel knew this. Israel also knew the Arabs had fled empty-handed, often half-clad as they leaped up from sleep and dashed blindly into the night, and were destitute. Inevitably some refugee would try to sneak back to his own home to see if it were safe to return, and if not, then to retrieve a few of his own belongings—his wife's shoes, his child's coat. The man was watched for by Israeli sentinels posted for that purpose. If they surprised him, as they always did, and if he fought in trying to get away, as he always did, then Israel had its next pretext. Israel could claim "Arab aggression against an Israeli settlement" and could justifiably make a "retaliatory attack" or a "punitive attack" and again advance its own borders. From Israel's point of view, it was a foolproof formula, used over and over again.

The fact that the "Israeli settlement" was actually across the line, newly planted on Arab territory, was ignored, was never mentioned, and is to this day unknown to the general American public.

That this was a planned program is shown by the fact that the attacks were not spontaneous and haphazard but came at six month intervals as spaced as the thumps of a metronome.

On October 14, 1953, a 600-man battalion of Israeli regulars using artillery, rifles, Sten guns, grenades and Bangalore torpedoes made a night attack on the Arab village of Qibya[6] a mile and a half inside Arab territory. They shot every man, woman, and child they could find. The grisly slaughter included even the animals. They dynamited the houses, the school, and the church (1954 *World Almanac,* pages 122-3).

Six months later, on March 28, 1954, uniformed Israeli regulars with heavy weapons attacked the Arab village of Nahalin.[7]

Six months later, on August 30, 1954, there was a wider sweep of 800 Israeli regulars who attacked three Arab villages[8] across the Line northwest of Jerusalem (1955 *World Almanac,* page 112).

Israel's area had now increased to 8,048 square miles (1955 *World Almanac*, page 359), thus leaving to Arab Palestine only 2,381 square miles.

While the original Partition Plan had allotted areas comparatively equal, Israel now held more than three times the space held by Arab Palestine.

What had the Arab governments done to protect themselves from this aggression and greedy seizure of territory? Incredible as it may seem, nothing. And this is easily explained. Although Israel had four Arab countries on its borders—Lebanon on the north, Syria on the northeast, Jordan on the east, and Egypt on the south, Israel had crossed only one border prior to 1955. That was Jordan's *because on that border*, as we have seen, *Israel was safe*.

But to continue: six months later,[9] on February 28, 1955, 200 Israeli regulars attacked across the Egyptian line at the Gaza Strip (1956 *World Almanac*, page 99).

This was something new, a first invasion across the border into Egyptian territory and a different effect immediately became apparent, for Egypt was a country with the odd belief that it had a perfect right to defend itself. Egypt began to buy guns.

Nevertheless, six months later, on August 22, 1955, an entire company of Israeli half-tracks brought havoc and devastation to Khan Yunis, again on the Egyptian border in Sinai[10] (*Time*, Sept. 12, 1955).

As September, 1955, ended, the reason for Israel's attacks on the Egyptian border became apparent. Israel brought in an oil well six miles from the Gaza Strip. "One of the main reasons the Israelis fought so hard to conquer the barren Negeb in the Palestine war was that they were sure they could find oil there" (*Time*, October 3, 1955).

In the meantime, Israel had quietly obtained Mystere jets from France.

Egypt, it was learned, was contracting to buy heavy arms and munitions from Czechoslovakia.

Arms for the Arabs! This gave an entirely new aspect to the whole situation. War, devastating and deadly, was a real and sudden and frightening possibility.

Surprising and horrifying as it was, it was a perfectly logical development. One marvels at the strange blindness, not only of Israel, with its peculiar astigmatism which sees solely its own objectives, but one wonders at the blindness of the Western world as well. We have complete newspaper coverage, prophetic pundits galore, and uninhibited perspective—why did not our statesmen realize that the Arabs, in response to Israel's ceaseless aggression, would finally get arms somewhere? One only wonders that they took so long.

With this public announcement, David ben-Gurion, Israel's new Premier, back in office, called for peace on November 2, 1955: "Without any prior conditions the Israeli government also is ready for a lasting and enduring peace settlement and for long-term political, economic and cultural cooperation between Israel and its neighbors."

At the very moment he was making this statement, an Israeli military coup must have been in preparation, for less than twelve hours later, on the night of November 2/3, Israeli army units *1000 strong* attacked Egyptian positions near El Auja in the Sinai Desert.[11]

"Israeli government spokesmen made no bones about

having struck far inside Egypt" (*Time,* Nov. 14, 1955).

On the same day, November 3, 1955, Secretary General Dag Hammarskjold of the UN offered a new peace plan.

The government of Israel replied with "complete support" of the UN Peace proposals "if the measures uphold Israel's rights and position in the tense El Auja (Nizana) area" and simultaneously called on the USA to sell Israel jet fighters and other weapons.

Despite the Egyptian arming, despite the "complete support" promised to the UN, Israel did not alter its course, as we shall see in the ensuing pages, but only intensified its program of regular-army, government-ordered attacks.

But now a disturbing element appeared. This, too, should have been foreseen, for native Palestinian Israelis were well aware of the Arabs' age-old custom of blood feud. Among the Arabs, this is a family obligation to avenge the unjust taking-of-life of any kinsman.

As 1955 moved toward autumn—"Small groups of Arab raiders carried the fight deep into Israel. Known as Al Fedayeen (Self Sacrificers) the sneaker-shod guerrillas are recruited from Palestinian Arab refugees and are thus adventurers without a country who know Israel's landscape, because it was once their own. Most of them are followers of the former Mufti of Jerusalem, who used to recruit men to fight both the British and the Jews. The Mufti has been living in Cairo" (*Time,* Sept. 12, 1955).

Impetus was given to the formation of the Al Fedayeen when the Senior Ulema at the 1000-year-old Al Azhar University in Cairo proclaimed a jihad or holy war against Israel (*Time,* Jan. 30, 1956). This proclamation was almost equivalent to a blanket "blessing of the church," and every Arab who had lost a member of his family, or a kinsman, felt freed of any further restraint.

With such obligations hanging over their heads, many of the refugees went into the desert, formed themselves into the bands of Self Sacrificers, and began crossing into Israel to take care of what they considered unfinished business.

Individual Arabs not in a position to get away and join the guerrilla bands acted on their own. "Many Arabs were killed inside Israel while trying to retrieve items from their former homes or harvests from the lands they had once possessed and to which they believed they still had legal title. Israel's 'get tough' policy to cope with Arab incursions did not pay off. Those infiltrators who escaped death or imprisonment were not intimidated—they armed themselves and went back for revenge" (*Violent Truce,* pages 10-11).

And so the storm gathered while the newspapers headlined "Middle East Crisis," and "Threat of War." Quickly a plan for peace was discussed. It called for Israel's giving up the Negev which they had seized five years previously and refused to give up when the Armistice terms were agreed in 1949. Israel was as firm in its refusal now to yield a foot of that territory. A returning correspondent told of quiet Israeli preparations for trouble, including partial mobilization, even before the attack on El Auja.

But to return to our now accelerated schedule.

Only six weeks after El Auja, on December 11/12, 1955, 300 armed Israeli infantrymen attacked three Syrian villages on the northeast shore of the Sea of Galilee. Fifty-six Syrians were left for dead. The Israeli government admitted it had ordered the attack.

In January, 1956, the UN Security Council unanimously condemned Israel for the attack on Syria.[12] "Shocking, heinous, outrageous," were some of the terms used by the members. Henry Cabot Lodge, Jr., US Delegate to the UN, declared it "a deed so out of proportion with the provocation that it cannot be accurately described as a retaliatory raid" (*Time,* Jan. 23, 1956). Syria asked sanctions against Israel and its expulsion from the UN.

But to continue—and show that practice makes perfect. In the *Saturday Evening Post* of February 18, 1956, Don Cook, in his article, "Tough Little Army," says: "The planned set-piece attacks which the *Israeli Army* has mounted against the Egyptians in the last twelve months—there have been five major ones—have more than proved that this army has a keen fighting edge. The attacks always are launched at night, and the army goes in with cold steel. One attack was carried out almost entirely by reservists under professional officers—the reservists had been called up only a few weeks before as a test of how well a reserve unit could perform. That was the attack in early November on El Auja-Nizana on the Negev border, and from an Israeli standpoint it was exactly according to plan and a complete success."

And when the 1956 spring planting was finished in Israel, what could the patriotic Land Army do to occupy itself profitably? In the May 29, 1956, issue of *Look,* that magazine's foreign editor, William Attwood, tells us: "The day I got to Cairo the Israelis opened fire on the Gaza Strip with artillery and 120-mm mortars, killing four Egyptian soldiers and *55 civilians* and wounding about *100 others.* Some of the shells came down on a hospital crowded with refugees. . . . *United Nations observers* told me that this was the fourth case of deliberate *military aggression* committed by the Israelis against Egypt in the past seven months."

UN Secretary, Dag Hammarskjold, rushed to the Middle East and won assurances of peace from antagonists. Israel's Foreign Minister, Moshe Sharett, announced: "Israel will not precipitate any major crisis" (*Time*, May 7, 1956).

Nor did they, all summer long, for greater deeds were in preparation. And of course the harvesting had to be done.

In August, Egypt's premier, Gamel Abdul Nasser, nationalized the Suez Canal, which lay entirely within Egypt, thus enraging its chief stockholders, Britain and France. Any nation angry at the Arabs was a potential ally of Israel. Here were two.

During September-October, as diversionary coverup to hide its preparations for a greater attack, Israel made four "reprisal" raids across the border. The biggest armed thrust was October 10 at Qalqilya[13] in Jordan, where UN observers later counted 48 Arab dead (*Time*, Oct. 22, 1956).

Israel's mobilization was now on such a full scale it could no longer be kept secret. President Eisenhower issued a strong warning to Israel's Premier Ben-Gurion against taking any "forceful initiative" and pledged aid to any victims of aggression in the Middle East.

In response, Israel's Ambassador, Abba Eban, replied flatly, "Israel will start no war."

The very next day the press reported an Israeli invasion of Egypt's Sinai Peninsula—"A preventive war to forestall imminent attack by Egypt." It had started on October 29, the day Mr. Eban had made his "*no* war" statement.

Israel did not send a boy to mill. Their 30,000-man

invasion force via tanks, jeeps, and half-tracks—and under cover of Mystere jets—lunged across the entire Sinai Peninsula and straight for the Suez Canal.

October 31, at dawn, Britain and France, with an army 50,000 strong (*Time*, Nov. 20, 1956), began an invasion of Egypt by planes, ships, paratroops, and land forces already quietly assembled in readiness on the Island of Cyprus.

In four days Israel took the Gaza Strip and the entire Peninsula of Sinai. As was her custom after each previous lightning land grab, she promptly agreed to a UN request for a cease-fire, thus neatly forestalling enemy retaliation.

After Britain and France had completed their destruction of Egyptian airfields and their seizure of the northern section of the Canal, they also agreed.

Egypt's appalling state of unpreparedness revealed only too plainly that it could not have been planning an "imminent attack" on Israel, nor in fact any aggression whatever.

Premier Ben-Gurion confidently pronounced the 1949 Armistice lines "dead" and laid claim to the whole of the Sinai Peninsula with its vast area of 23,000 square miles. Britain's Eden, certainly not to be outdone by such a small nation as Israel, demanded that Egypt withdraw 100 miles from its own Egypt-Israeli frontiers and leave the "protection" of the Suez Canal to Britain and France (*Time*, Nov. 19, 1956). The utter complaisance of the three allies could not have been greater.

In rapid succession that complaisance received a couple of knockout blows—the first truly horrifying: Russia issued a flat ultimatum that Britain-France-Israel get out of Egypt immediately or she, Russia, would "permit"

200,000 Russian "volunteers" to go to Egypt's rescue (*Time,* Nov. 12, 1956); and Red China chimed in, mentioning the number of "volunteers" she would "permit" as 250,000. The next blow, while milder, was far more humiliating. The attack had been cleverly timed to take place just before the US presidential election on November 6. Mr. Eden's theory was that Mr. Eisenhower would keep silent about Israel's aggression for fear of alienating the Jewish-American vote and continue to keep silent about British-French aggression for fear of losing his NATO allies.

Mr. Eden misjudged his man. President Eisenhower, without a moment's hesitation, and *before* election, forthrightly condemned not only Israel but Britain and France as well. He served blunt notice that US commitments of arms and gasoline to NATO did not include assistance in Middle East aggression.

He was equally blunt in warning Russia to keep out.

With that very fear of Russian intervention in the back of every delegate's mind, the UN ordered the three aggressors to withdraw from Egypt "forthwith."

Never before in history had any voice given an *order* to Britain "forthwith." Mr. Eden promptly relinquished to others the tough job of extricating his government from the frightful mess he'd got it into and flew to the Caribbean. Despite the fact that the saving of the Middle East and the salvaging of NATO, two Herculean tasks, were gratuitously dumped into Mr. Eisenhower's lap, the British press released itself in an orgy of uncontrolled savagery aimed at the USA.

When the UN and the US continued adamant in their demand for Israel's withdrawal from Sinai, and Israel was forced reluctantly to agree to do so, Mrs. Golda

Meir, Israel's Foreign Minister, calmly suggested that Sinai be taken from Egypt and made neutral territory. "Sinai," said she in an interview November 29, 1956, "is unoccupied and always has been."

Mrs. Meir displays either an astounding ignorance of history or a cool assumption of the public's ignorance. From the earliest historical times,[14] Sinai has been a part of Egypt. That nation was operating copper mines there before the Exodus. There is a native population. They cultivate date groves in the southern valleys and graze their flocks along the northern water courses. The Wady el Arish in northeastern Sinai is and has been throughout history the "River of Egypt."

This is the situation to date.

But the basic cause of the Middle East conflict—Israel vs. Arab—remains. Its chief feature? Israeli aggression. That we know now. As the figures show, that small nation has steadily extended its territory from the original 5,500 square miles assigned to it—first to 7,100; then to 7,800; then to 8,048 square miles. This was done in the brief space of 8 years. And now it invades a neighbor nation to seize and make every effort to hold the vast expanse of Sinai with its area of approximately 23,000 square miles and its, as yet undetermined, mineral possibilities—especially as regards fissionable materials.

How does any nation accomplish a gain in territory if not by pushing across the line and taking more land? One does not gain territory by staying on one's own side of the fence.

We cannot doubt that the Israel government ordered these acts of aggression, for, according to General Benneke's report of November 29, 1953, to the UN Security Council, sixteen of the resolutions condemning Israel by the Israel-Jordan Mixed Armistice Commission were for attacks "carried out by Israeli military forces."

And the UN Security Council itself, even before the invasion of Sinai, had condemned Israel four times in the following listed Resolutions: S/2157, May 18, 1951; S/3139, November 24, 1953; S/3378, March 29, 1955; and S/3538, January 19, 1956.[15]

Israel claims self-defense, but if the fighting were really in self-defense against invaders, would it not occur at the border or on the Israeli side of the Line? Why do these slaughters of entire Arab villages always take place across the line on the Arab side?

What is the record on the other side of the ledger? What of the Arabs? Have they ever attacked Israel by government order? Has any Arab army ever attempted to invade Israel?

Incredible as it may seem, no. The only reason this record seems so terribly one-sided is because it *is* one-sided. "No Arab State has ever been brought before the Security Council for an attack by its armed forces on Israeli-held territory" (*The Record of Israel at the United Nations* by Fayez A. Sayegh, Counsellor of the Yemen Delegation to the UN and the US and Deputy Director of the Arab States Delegation Office, page 87).

But the information from the UN is really unnecessary, for the proof—the irrefutable proof—of "whose guilt" lies in the statistics; and figures do not lie. There stands the damning evidence, the difference between Israel's original 5,500 square miles of the original allotment and the 8,048 square miles held now. And the amount may be even greater than this, for—strangely enough—Israel's area is not reported in the 1956 *World Almanac.*

But perhaps the means by which this gain has been

achieved—a spring attack and an autumn attack—is the most spine chilling feature of the whole Palestinian picture. What fantastic program is this which sends its young men out to kill the neighbors every six months in the slack time after the winter sowing and again after the summer harvest? This is a program as terrible as a regular hunting season, a twice-yearly open season on the human race.

Its object, the driving out of a million human beings, adds to the nightmare quality of this fantastic chain of events which make a tale more bizarre than any horror story ever written by Poe.

Israel has now taken most of Palestine. But at no time was possession of Palestine in its entirety ever intended by the planners of the Partition. Dispossession of the Arab population was never contemplated in the wildest dreams of the UN and Mr. Truman, nor—God forbid—of the American People, our taxpayers, who have to date given $404,000,000 to Israel.

What of the American Jews? Do they know this terrifying record of Israel's massacres? Is it what they intended? Here also, God forbid.

No, they, more than any other Americans, have been singled out as a segment and subjected to a continuous stream of lecturers who come from Israel for the very crass purpose of getting money. To accomplish this, the speakers have developed a technique known as the old one-two. First they speak of constructive, idealistic projects in Israel. Then they point out that Israel is in deadly danger from without and elaborate on this in order to stir up the emotions of their listeners. By such means and methods Israel has obtained from American Jews the staggering sum of $1,032,000,000.

Do our Jewish fellow Americans know they are actively financing a program of assassination and grand theft?

Again no. The true facts have been hidden from them, and well hidden, by their own particular sources of information. Instead, in addition to outright propaganda, they have been indoctrinated by subtle means, by implication, and by the dissemination of seemingly reliable misinformation. As an example, one columnist recently made the apparently proper suggestion that Israel make her crooked borders easier to "defend" by straightening them to run in a direct line along the Jordan-Dead Sea. Did he not know that to do such a thing Israel would have to jump clear across to the farther side, thus annexing the whole of Arab Palestine? Or did he assume the casual reader would not know it?

But American Jews have been nurtured in the same ideals of peace and brotherhood as we other Americans. Never, no matter how they are propagandized, would they knowingly finance the slaughter of any section of the human race.

No, that is not what they intended, nor we, nor Mr. Truman, nor the UN.

They created the State of Israel for a home where oppressed peoples could be at peace. Instead, it has been used as a base from which to launch seizure and terror.

The most valuable commodity in the world today being good faith, perhaps the most discouraging feature of all is the deadly purpose behind the camouflage of fair words, the steadily intensifying drive, the increase in the size and scope of Israel's military operations, the growth of aggression from small beginnings to 30,000 troop attacks.

And the climax in disillusionment is reached when we see and hear Israel's Ambassador, Mr. Abba Eban, stand and voice his country's acceptance of peace proposals while at the same moment the Israeli army is secretly mobilizing and starting to invade another country. This is identical with the methods employed, not indeed by the Communists, but by the Japanese on the day of Pearl Harbor.

What reason can possibly motivate Israel in this strange course? What of Israel itself? Its leaders know they are engaged in aggression and theft of territory. How do they justify themselves? And have they, by means of indoctrination, built up some theory of justification in the minds of their followers? What do they tell them?

Do they tell them that Israel has a political right to all this territory because it was once the Kingdom of David and Solomon?

Do American Jews, to still their doubts and questionings, tell themselves the same thing?

And do Christian, church-going Americans—when they read of Israel's slaughters and the UN condemnations—pause dubiously and wonder if it is true that maybe Israel does have some right to all of Palestine?

What is the real answer? What is the right thing for us to do? And for our government? And for the American Jews?

We shall never know until we examine the question of Israel's political right to Palestine. We want an answer to this question—*Does Israel have a political right, under international law, to the land of Palestine?*

Political Rights

WRITERS ON Middle East history call Palestine the crossroads of the ancient world. This is no mere figure of speech. It was and is a real crossroads, and therein lay—and now lies—the root of the trouble.

Then, as now, the surrounding picture changed as old nations fell and new ones rose, but throughout the whole of ancient history the great and densely populated Egypt of the Pharaohs was on the south. Palestine's east line joined with a row of small neighboring countries—Edom, Moab, Ammon, and Gilead—while the great Arabian desert beyond was filled with countless thousands of nomadic tribesmen. And farther east, beyond the great desert, the rich nations of Assyria and Babylonia flourished throughout the centuries on the Tigris and Euphrates Rivers.[16] At times the Amorites on the immediate north in what is now Syria were powerful, and at one time Mitanni beyond sprang into prominence. For several hundred years the Hittites were northwest in Asia Minor. West lay Crete with its splendid culture, and across the strait of the Hellespont on the mainland of Europe lay the land later known as Greece, with its adjacent Isles of the Sea, their ships full of rip-snorting sea rovers who cruised the Mediterranean and could invade Palestine from that direction.

Palestine, the ancient Land of Canaan, was in the center, between all these—the corridor, the passageway, the sea outlet, the crossroads across which all the surrounding nations could jump at each other, perhaps annihilate each other. By taking and holding the crossroads, any one of them could also bar all the others out of this highway intersection.

To gain control of Canaan, the vital four-way crossing, the surrounding nations invaded and conquered it in turn from the south, the east, the north and the west, the stronger nations succeeding the weaker in a continuous stream, sometimes surging back and forth in a tug-of-war, but flowing in from the earliest known times right down in an uninterrupted sequence to the present. Each nation, as now, tried to get a toehold, then complete control, then establish a political claim to Palestine and make the claim stick permanently.

Always, between foreign conquests, the settled inhabitants of the Land of Canaan, the Canaanites, tried to set up their own independent government and to stay free. They never succeeded, as we shall see. Always, *because they were a crossroads,* some of the neighboring Great Powers seized them and established sovereign rule. Throughout its long history, the *only* sovereign rule of any length or consequence was by conquerors from without who either ruled from without or moved in bodily onto the Canaanites.

Of all these various conquerors and sovereign rulers, which one established the best political right to Palestine?

As a preface, we state the position of the present civilized world: any dispute over property, whether individual or national, should be settled, not by one claimant taking it forcibly from the other individual or nation with a shotgun, but by due process of law, by civil litigation in a courtroom for the individual; and for nations, civil litigation before the International World Court, with the evidence presented in an orderly manner and the litigants, whether individual or national, abiding by the decision.

This evidence, like a real estate abstract, should show a complete history of the property's ownership from the beginning.

What is the story of Palestine's ownership? What does the abstract show?

Here, in the following pages, is a brief but complete historical record of Palestine from the earliest known times right down to and including the present.

Going back to earliest times, scientists tell us that prehistoric skulls found at Carmel in Palestine represent a mixed race intermediate between *Neanderthal Man* and *Homo sapiens*.[17] They say it is within the realm of possibility that *Homo sapiens* himself came from somewhere else and thus started Palestine's deadly cycle of conquest and reconquest even before history began, as one race invaded the other, conquered it and united with it. If we let our imagination play, we may reconstruct a lively and highly entertaining scene—either the *Neanderthal Man* dragging the *Homo sapiens* maiden into a cave by the hair of her head, or, what would be stranger and still more hilarious, a *Homo sapiens* Casanova struggling valiantly to drag a hefty *Neanderthal* Amazon into the cave by the hair of her head. At any rate, *Neanderthal Man* disappeared, and *Homo sapiens* was the survivor.

Archaeologists tell us that the inhabitants of 50,000 to 20,000 years ago lived in the open during the warm, dry periods, and in caves during the cold, wet periods where their fossils and stone hand-axes have been found.[18]

Tools and utensils in the successively later levels of excavation indicate that the primitive peoples gradually became more adept in their means of existence and survival as time went on. To their stone hand axes and fist hatchets they added other implements, flint arrowheads, as they learned to hunt effectively, flint sickle blades with hafts of bone as they learned to reap more expeditiously, pick-like hoes, pestles and mortars, bone pins and awls. From fossil bones we learn that the dog is indeed man's oldest friend, for it was the first animal they were able to domesticate.

At this now advanced stage, what kind of people were these primitives? Little fellows about five feet tall. Their skeletons and the shape of their fossil skulls indicate Semitic-Hamitic stock, so the experts tell us.[19] This agrees well with the Biblical statement that the Canaanites were the first people in Palestine. Canaan was the son of Ham— and Ham and Shem were brothers with skulls probably as alike as two Palestinian pomegranates.

So this country as history first knows it, was peopled by Canaanites and named the Land of Canaan. But the inhabitants were also known by the name of the town or valley in which they lived—just as Americans in Los Angeles are sometimes referred to as Angelenos, so were the Canaanites in the city of Jebus (Jerusalem) called Jebusites.

The Canaanites advanced in the arts and crafts and learned to build houses whose levelled clay floors were finished with lime plaster beautifully painted and polished.[20] Of course the houses were clustered together near a water supply—a spring or a well, or on the banks of a stream.

We may be fairly proud of these and the other nearby

originators of civilization, for with no previous knowledge to guide them, they discovered soft copper about 4,000 B.C.[21] and within the next thousand years learned to combine it with tin to make the warmly rich and beautiful bronze, a discovery probably more important to the world at that time than the discovery of nuclear fission is to us now, for it introduced the science of metallurgy and gave these primitive peoples hard, sharp, and durable tools and weapons.

It also made them more dangerous to each other. Just as we erect an arctic radar screen against our potential enemies now, the ancients built massive walls to encircle and protect their towns—Beth-shan and Jericho, and Jebus (Jerusalem) and Megiddo—names heard with an odd sense of recognition dating from our childhood days in Sunday School class.

Archeological remains of the period in the form of goods traded show that commerce was brisk between Egypt and Babylonia via the Canaanite crossroads.

The importance of the intersection was recognized even at that early date. Egypt, like Mexico on our south, was the nearer, so the powerful Pharaohs of the First and Second Egyptian Dynasties extended their domain to include Canaan, which became a colonial possession.[22] This was about 2800 B.C., and from this distance we can recognize the first colonial administrator to reach and take charge of the crossroads—he is a fine-boned, wiry, brown-bodied Egyptian in a white linen kilt.

But other points of the compass were to be heard from, and, as the years passed, nomads pushed into the Canaanite corridor, disturbing the peace and prompting thoughts of rebellion among the settled population.

Writing had been invented, and Egypt inscribed on vases and statuettes the names of potential colonial rebels in a set of inscriptions called the Execration Texts, names which included some of the peoples of Canaan.[23]

Historians believe the 20th and 19th centuries B.C. correspond to the Patriarchal Age of the Bible and that the Hebrew or Habiru tribesman named Abram may have come up from Babylonian Chaldea and drifted into the Land of Canaan at about this time.[24]

Although Egypt still claimed Canaan as part of her empire, some of the nomads from the north who were called Hyksos disregarded this and shifted south to enter the Land of Canaan.[25] About 1710 B.C. they knocked the little Egyptian colonial governor on the head. If we may judge by a statue in the British Museum, the Hyksos administrator who took over the crossroads was long-nosed, thin-lipped and big-eared.[26]

The empire of the Hyksos lasted in Canaan from about 1710 to 1480 B.C. and left literally thousands of inscribed seals everywhere.

In 1480 B.C. the kilted, brown Egyptians, coming up from the south, drove the Hyksos out of Canaan and once again took possession of the crossroads to hold it this time for a well authenticated 130 years.[27]

Then the Pharaoh Akhnaten of Egypt lost the empire himself. He believed in only one God and not in the many Egyptian gods, which belief to the Egyptians was manifest heresy. The empire fell to pieces, and in the general confusion, Egypt's foreign colonies, including Canaan, got free. The date for this (Albright Chronology) is 1350 B.C.

But the city kings of Canaan, each too weak to stay free, were easy prey for the next attackers from another direction.

These aggressors were easy to predict, for they had a new and up-to-the-minute weapon of war, a cold and deadly killer, the last word, the latest discovery which would influence all subsequent history up to and including this modern stainless steel moment. It was iron. And up northwest, in Asia Minor, the peak-headed, barrel-bodied Hittites had it. In their mountain mine-caves they smelted it and worked it secretly by elaborate ritual formulas which would impart magical powers of strength and self-preservation to the owner of each and every sword and dagger.[28]

Armed thus, the Hittites set out and took most of the territory belonging to their neighbor Mittani. The Assyrians on the east took the rest of it, and Mittani disappeared.

The victorious Hittites then turned south and took Syria (the land of the Amorites). Then they took Canaan, and the crossroads administrator became a Hittite wearing a hood-like helmet and a broad belt fitting as snugly round his middle as a hoop around a barrel.

Egypt had gone to pieces temporarily, but she got hold of herself, and about 1290 B.C. (Albright Chronology), her most famous Pharaoh—Ramses the Great—roared up from the south to meet the Hittites head on in a mighty battle at Kadesh in Amor and succeeded in retaking the southern part of the Canaanite corridor. The victory was limited, for the iron-fisted Hittites still held Amor.

History then began to gather itself for a supreme effort, and events which would reshape the entire world of the ancient Mediterranean were now in the making. Fighting men and nations wanted not only the magic iron, but conquest—lands, wealth, trade routes. They swept forward.[29]

As the movements of peoples farther away began to affect Canaan, the perimeter of the crossroads was enlarged. Farther to the west and north, the Balkan and

Black Sea peoples slid down into Greece, where the big, blond Achaean adventurers took to the sea, crossed the Hellespont, and attacked the Phrygians at Troy. Rip-snorters from all the islands of the eastern Mediterranean got out their oars, hoisted sail, and their war galleys swarmed all along the coasts and far to the southeast corner of the Mediterranean to attack Egypt.

On land, everyone began to move—a mass migration by two-wheeled wagon—and the world surged like a tide. Suddenly, about 1200 B.C., the Hittite Empire was wiped out (how is not known), with only its remnants surviving in Amor. The tide rolled south into that land, and the Amorites picked up and began to move too.

Egypt repulsed the attempted invasion, drove the invaders back, and it is thought that at this time the Habiru, or Hebrew, descendants of Abraham in bondage in Egypt, escaped in the general confusion and fled to the desert of Sinai.

Wandering there in the eternal search for pasture, the Hebrews grazed their flocks forward, and the desert tribes already there did the same, inching toward the grasslands of Canaan whenever possible.

Egypt had also defeated the Sea-raiders and pushed them away. One contingent of these raiders, the Philistines, backed up along the coast of Canaan as Egypt chased them up from the south.

So Canaan had Egypt still trying to maintain its hold from that direction while the Amorites closed in from the north, the desert tribes (including the Hebrews) from the east, and the rip snorting sea raiders from the west—all making a rush for the crossroads![30] Often as the Canaanites had been caught in the middle, seldom had they been squeezed so hard.

Who won the race? Those who happened to be nearest: the Philistine warriors whose trademark was a crown-like circlet of feathers, from the west, by inundation; and the bearded Hebrews, or Israelites, as they now called themselves, from the eastern desert, by sporadic attack and infiltration.

It is believed by some authorities that the Israelites made their Exodus from Egypt about 1224 B.C.[31] And that after wandering forty years in the desert, they, in the psychological moment when everything had gone to pieces, invaded Canaan about 1184 B.C. This was at exactly the same time Troy is believed to have fallen (an odd coincidence little noticed by historians).

Of the two foreign invaders, the feather-crowned Philistines[32] were the stronger, for they defeated the bearded Israelites and even put them in bondage. ("And the Lord delivered them into the hands of the Philistines forty years," Judges 13:1.)

The Philistines also left a lasting mark, their name, on the crossroads. It ceased to be called Canaan and came in time to be known as Palestine. Now, 3000 years later, after many changes of allegiance and sovereignty, it is still most familiarly known as Palestine.

However, neither the Philistines nor the Israelites were able to establish control over the native inhabitants in their walled cities. Most historians list Egypt as the ruler until the end of the reign of Rameses III, about 1154 B.C., after which Egyptian rule seemed to become one in name only.[33]

Canaan was in a state of tug-of-war between the two invaders from without, the Philistines and the Israelites, until about 1000 B.C. That is the date given for the Israelite King David's taking of Jerusalem.[34] He defeated the

Philistines, conquered Canaan, and went on eventually to conquer the row of small neighboring nations east of Palestine (Edom, Moab, Ammon, and Gilead). He set up an independent kingdom, and the crossroads ruler was now a cloaked and bearded warrior-poet.

David ruled, in all, forty years (seven as a city-king at Hebron and thirty-three years at Jerusalem after the establishment of the kingdom);[35] and his son Solomon ruled for forty years,[36] giving the Kingdom of David and Solomon a complete life span of seventy-three years.

Then it ended. After the death of Solomon, about 927 B.C., the kingdom fell apart. The small neighboring nations on the east got free, and Palestine itself was split into two countries hostile to each other. The tribes of Judah and Benjamin formed the kingdom of Judah on the south, and the remaining ten tribes formed the kingdom of Israel on the north.

Each one was too weak to stand alone. Egypt came up, invaded Judah, and sacked Solomon's new temple at Jerusalem. Ben-Hadad of Syria on the north annexed part of Israel's territory, then formed an alliance with Israel against Judah. Desperately, Judah appealed to far-off Assyria.

The black-bearded and brutal Assyrians needed no second invitation but came over from the distant northeast, devastated and conquered the whole of Israel in 722 B.C. and carried the Ten Tribes away into captivity (Albright Chronology). Thus the section of the Hebrews known as Israel disappeared.

Judah tried to survive but was too small. Nebuchadnezzar of Babylon came up from the distant east, invaded Judah, and, in 586 B.C., destroyed Jerusalem,[37] carried the Judeans also into captivity, and left a Babylonian star-gazer to manage the crossroads.

But in 538 B.C., the Babylonians themselves saw the handwriting on the wall at the feast of Belshazzar, as the conquering Persians from still farther to the northeast marched in and took over the Babylonian Empire. This included Palestine.[38]

The lenient, light-worshiping Persians allowed some of the Babylonian captive Jews to return to Jerusalem and rebuild it. The Persians, who were of Aryan extraction, sat on their Persian carpets and administered the crossroads until the next invader came, this time from the west.

He was Alexander the Great, leading a victorious army of Greeks to conquer and take the Middle East as far as Persia, including Palestine, which was taken in 330 B.C.[39]

By far the most civilized people of the ancient world, the Greeks were sculptors and architects, scientists and mathematicians, poets and philosophers. And so the handsome athlete at the crossroads wore the *chlamys*[40] of the Greek soldier, but he probably wrote poetry as he watched the world go by.

From these newcomers, the young and eager of the Middle East learned to reason, to think along new lines, to realize that the world was full of dazzling ideas—and, consequently, to depart from age-old tradition—a departure which infuriated the Jewish elders.

Alexander the Great had taken Egypt and Syria, and when he died in 323 B.C. his Middle East Empire was divided between two of his generals: Ptolemy, who got Egypt; and Seleucus, who got Syria. And these generals quarreled over Palestine, which lay between them. Ptolemy of Egypt got it. But in 200 B.C. it fell to the Seleucids of Syria.

Division brought weakness and dissension, and the Jews of Palestine seized the opportunity to revolt under their High Priest Simon Maccabaeus in 142 B.C. However, this date for Maccabean independence is debatable, for the historian Josephus (*Antiquities*, XIII, x, i) says that Simon's successor, John Hyrcanus (134-105 B.C.), was the one who revolted. And the independence itself is debatable. At that time Judea was not only still claimed by the Seleucids but by one Diodotus Tryphon, a military adventurer who had set himself up as king, and the Jews were paying tribute to said Tryphon.[41]

The Jewish attempt at independence was short lived, for in 70 B.C. they were overrun and conquered by a new and apparently powerful enemy, Armenia, coming down the north road.[42]

It is hardly worth while describing the Armenians, for they proved to be only a flash in the pan when a real power, Rome, arrived from the west, the invader coming from across the sea, from farther afield than ever before.

The Roman Empire, based in what is now Italy, had by this time become the colossus of the ancient world and now proceeded to conquer most of that world. Roman citizens were go-getters with the technical knowledge to build and organize anything, anywhere.

In 63 B.C. the Roman general, Pompey, took Jerusalem,[43] and while a helmeted Roman legionnaire stood at the traffic intersection, Rome set up a puppet king, an Edomite named Herod, to rule Palestine, which in time became the Roman province of Judea.

The hated Herod levied confiscatory taxes, impressed labor, and, aping Rome, built enormous and costly public improvements, including new city walls and a great temple for the Jews at Jerusalem. It was into this world that Jesus was born.

Unfortunately, the Roman emperors of this particular period had little regard for traditional Roman justice and equity. Mostly they were brutal tyrants, and in two instances, actually madmen, while their local puppet kings and procurators in the provinces and colonies were often equally brutal and tyrannical.

As a result, the provinces of Judea fought two bitter and bloody, but unsuccessful, wars of revolt—the first in A.D. 70 and the second in A.D. 135.

The final Roman punishment was to destroy Jerusalem completely and thoroughly disperse the entire Jewish population to the far parts of the Roman Empire.[44]

Rome rebuilt Jerusalem and renamed it Aelia Capitolina, and, at first, no Jew could live there or even enter the city (*Syrian Pageant* by W. T. F. Castle, page 73). Thus official Jewish connection with Palestine came to an end in A.D. 135 and was non-existent for the next 1800 years.

Roman rule in Judea continued for centuries, first from Rome (63 B.C. to A.D. 395)[45]; then (A.D. 395 to A.D. 614) from Constantinople (Byzantium), the capital of the Eastern Roman Empire, continued at the crossroads until A.D. 614, when the Persians from the east attacked and took Jerusalem. That is the convenient date usually given by historians for the Persian subjugation of all Judea.

The conquest was for only a brief 14 years until 628, when the Persians, in an exchange of conquests and prisoners, returned Palestine to Rome.[46]

But both nations felt a chill wind creeping in from the wide Arabian desert. It brought clouds of dust from the thundering surge of thousands of nomad horsemen and the voice of the Arab leader Mohammed proclaiming in tones of doom: "The heavens shall be rent in sunder!" They were.

In A.D. 638, the Arab followers of Mohammed took the

entire Roman Empire of the Middle East, the Palestine crossroads included.[47] In time, they extended their rule far along both sides of the Mediterranean and even crossed the Strait of Gibraltar into Spain.

The brown man at the four-corners now wore a desert cloak and headcloth.

By the thousands, the desert Arabs settled in Palestine. They converted the Canaanites (who, through all the changing sovereignties—although much diluted by foreign blood—still formed the backbone of the rural population) to the Moslem faith, intermarried with them; and the language and customs of the crossroads in time became Arabic; the architecture in time, Arabic; the population itself, partially Arabic.[48]

The Arabic followers of Mohammed called themselves Moslems and their religious world Islam. From this time forward, until the end of World War I (with the exception of the relatively brief period of the Crusades), the crossroads was to be under Moslem domination—sometimes from one quarter, sometimes from another, depending on where the Caliph lived and whether he was one of the Omayyads of Damascus, one of the Abassids of Baghdad, or one of the Fatimates of Cairo.[49] Sometimes the rule was even by another race than the Arab. But from whatever quarter and by whatever people, the control remained Moslem.

Under the Arabs, religious persecution finally developed, and by A.D. 1000, the Christian followers of Jesus were obliged to carry ten-pound crosses, and the few scattered Jews still remaining in Palestine were required to wear black garments and bells round their necks.[50]

About A.D. 1085, Malik Shah made Palestine a part of

the empire of the Seljuk Turks which had risen to rule in the northeast in Persia, Iraq, and Anatolia.[51] The Turks were Moslem, as were the residents at the crossroads; so the change was merely an external one in which Arab desert architecture included the tiled domes of the Seljuks. Religious persecution continued.[52]

This prompted Christians, still farther afield in Europe, to organize an army and try to free the Holy Land from Moslem domination. The movement was called a Crusade, and the army of Crusaders, coming from the west across the sea,[53] took Jerusalem in A.D. 1099. And now, oddly enough, the Crusader in chain mail who directed traffic at the crossroads was either a Dutchman, or a Frenchman, or an Englishman, or an Italian, or possibly a German.

By means of constant reinforcements through later Crusades, the Europeans maintained limited and uncertain occupation for almost two hundred years.

In the later part of this period, one of the most glamorous figures in history, Saladin, the brave and gallant leader of the Moslem armies, who had come down from the northeast out of the mountain of Kurdistan, dealt the Crusaders their death sentence. This was their defeat at the battle of Hattin, July 4, 1187.

But they did not expire finally until after Tatar hordes called Khwarizmians descended on the crossroads from the Aral Sea and took Jerusalem,[54] massacring thousands, and were followed close by Mongol hordes from still farther east under Hulagu Khan, the grandson of Genghis Khan, who brought fire and horror and death and destruction to the Middle East.

This was something the Moslems had not counted on. Another contingent of them called the Mamelukes came up from the south, from Cairo in Egypt, and helped the Crusaders defeat the Mongols in A.D. 1260.[55]

Eventually the Mamelukes turned on their erstwhile Christian allies and finally, in A.D. 1291, they expelled them from the Middle East for good and all, and the last remnants of the disorganized Crusader armies trickled back to Europe.[56]

The Moslem Mamelukes from the south (Egypt, for the umpteenth time) now ruled the crossroads.

Next, down from the northwest came the Ottoman branch of the Turks to defeat the Mamelukes of Egypt and gain possession not only of Palestine but, via that corridor, to move on and conquer Egypt itself, then extend their rule along both sides of the Mediterranean, as the Arabs had done before them. This was about the time Columbus discovered America.

Suleiman the Magnificent took charge in Palestine and rebuilt Jerusalem, where his great walls stand to this day. The Ottoman Turk regime, 1517-1918, was a continuation of the Moslem, and the language of the country continued to be Arabic, as it had been since A.D. 638.

But Turkish rule became corrupt and tyrannical, and the local Arab population in Palestine was ready for revolt by 1914, when World War I began.

In the meantime, another element had been added to the crossroads picture. The Jews had had no part in the political history of Palestine since their final dispersion of A.D. 135, and historians estimate their maximum number in the whole of Palestine at the beginning of the 19th century at fewer than 10,000. Notwithstanding this, the movement called Zionism was organized in Middle Europe with the aim of creating a home in Palestine for the Jewish people, and Jewish immigration was activated in the latter part of the century with the largest settlement made at a village called Tel Aviv, near the Mediterranean.

World War I began in 1914. Turkey, the ruler in Palestine, joined with Germany against Britain and France and was defeated in 1918. The Turks lost Palestine; their rule came to an end and was replaced by a British Mandate, 1923, and the man in the fez was replaced at the crossroads by a British Tommy.

The Arabs of all the Middle-East States—Lebanon, Syria, Iraq, Trans-Jordan, and Palestine—expected independence in return for their help to Britain during the war. The Zionists also, in return for their help to Britain, demanded an independent state in Palestine.

But if Palestine were wholly and independently Arab, the Israel demands could not be met; and if Israel demands were met, the Arabs' could not be. So the UN sawed the child in two. They decreed the end of the British Mandate in 1948, and the Palestine crossroads country was divided between the Zionists and the Arabs. The Zionists, who had infiltrated from the west, were awarded the west half, which they named Israel; and the east half was annexed by the small state of Trans-Jordan (beyond the Dead Sea), which renamed itself the Hashemite Kingdom of Jordan. The United Nations declared Jerusalem an international zone.

The Palestine Arabs were enraged at having half their country taken from them and given to Israel; and the Israelis were enraged at not getting Jerusalem, which they demanded.

War broke out; the Israelis advanced, took additional Palestine territory, evicting almost a million Palestinian refugees, and tried to take Jerusalem but failed.

The United Nations finally succeeded in getting a cessation of hostilities and drew an armistice line along the battlefront. There the matter now stands, with the line being constantly violated in crisis after crisis and no peace settlement in sight.

To add to this stupendous record of multiple ownership and make the problem still more urgent, Palestine is today a crossroads to an even greater degree than ever before. The radius it draws from is enormously expanded, and the Middle East is now a four-way intersection for the criss-crossing airlanes of the world. Planes from the western nations fly in over the Mediterranean; Egypt and Africa come up from the south; Iraq and Iran, Pakistan and India from the east; and Turkey and Russia have a near approach from the north. All gravitate centripetally toward the crossroads vortex, and the avaricious among them scheme more subtly and psychologically than their ancient predecessors dreamed.

Should global war break out, the Great Powers would fight far more furiously for this spot, trying not only to reach the crossroads a jump ahead of each other, but to grab and hold it.

For this reason a permanent settlement is imperative, with some UN agreement among the World Powers to respect the crossroads and keep it inviolate.

Let us then evaluate the evidence we have collected and try to determine who really has a right to Palestine.

The political right to any territory is determined by such fundamentals as priority of occupation, length and continuity of rule, recent ownership, and the racial character of the present population.

After the original Canaanite city-states, Palestine was almost continuously occupied by outsiders. We may best grasp our facts if we reduce them to figures.

Rulers of Palestine	*Date of Rule*	*Length of Rule–Years*
	B.C.	
Canaanites	First settlers	?
Egypt	Indefinite	Indefinite
Hyksos	1710-1480	230
Egypt (authenticated)	1480-1350	130
Hittite	1350-1290	60
Egypt	1290-1154	136
Local (Canaanites, Philistines and Jews)	1154-1000	154
Jews (David and Solomon)	1000- 927	73
Jews (Israel, Ten Tribes)	927- 722	
Jews (Judah)	927- 586	
Jews (widest spread of dates)	1000- 586	414
Babylonia	586- 538	48
Persia	538- 330	208
Greece	330- 323	7
Egyptians (Ptolemies)	323- 200	123
Seleucids (Syria)	200- 142	57

Rulers of Palestine	*Date of Rule*	*Length of Rule–Years*
Jews (Maccabees, partial only)	142- 70	72
Seleucids (Tryphon, partial only)	142- 70	72
Armenia	70- 63	7
Rome (Western and Eastern Empires)	63 B.C.– A.D. 614	677
	A.D.	
Persia	614- 628	14
Rome	628- 638	10
Arab (Moslem)	638-1085	447
Turks (Seljuk: Moslem)	1085-1099	14
Crusaders (partial only)	1099-1291	192
Seljuk and Arab (Moslem, partial only)	1099-1291	192
Egypt (Mamelukes: Moslem)	1291-1517	226
Turks (Ottoman: Moslem)	1517-1918	401
Great Britain	1923-1948	25
Jews (Israel, partial, west only)	1948-1957	9
Arab (Jordan, partial, east only)	1948-1957	9

By a process of quick elimination, we weed out the defunct who left no known heirs (Hyksos, Hittites, Philistines, Seleucids, Seljuks); the brief (Babylonia, Greece, Armenia, Great Britain); the partial or divided rule (Seleucid-Maccabee, Crusader-Arab, modern Israel-Jordan); and the short-term second attempts (Persia and Rome).

Next we eliminate the one whose term of rule was not the first, nor the latest, nor long enough to compete seriously with the long-termers: Persia, 208 years.

This leaves us the long-termers, some of whom may also have priority of rule or recent possession and rule. One or two of their names may surprise us.

Egypt was the first outside Great Power to establish sovereignty over the crossroads. If we omit entirely her first long but indefinite terms of occupation as mentioned by Dr. Albright and add only her two early datable terms of 266 years to the later 123-year and the 226-year rule, we arrive at a total of 615 years for Egypt.

The length of the original Jewish rule in Palestine is usually reckoned by them from Saul to the Babylonian captivity. But Saul's early reign had no real sovereignty over the land, which was largely under the control of the Canaanites and Philistines, as it was during the 7 years of David's reign at Hebron before he defeated the Philistines, conquered Canaan, and took Jerusalem. The extended kingdom of David and Solomon, on which the Zionists base their territorial demands, endured for only about 73 years—from approximately 1000 B.C. to about 927 B.C.—which would put it in the short-term class. Thereafter, neither Israel nor Judah had true independence, for both "paid tribute" to one or another outside Great Power, and each owed its continued existence to the protection of that Great Power. After the conquest of the Ten Tribes of Israel by Assyria in 722 B.C., the rump kingdom of Judah actually occupied an area of about 50 by 75 miles, a much smaller plot of ground than that now held by modern Israel, and equivalent in size to a 50-mile wide patch of our coast reaching from Los Angeles to Oceanside. But if we allow independence to the *entire life* of the ancient Jewish kingdoms, from David's conquest of Canaan in 1000 B.C. to the wiping out of Judah in 586 B.C., we arrive at a 414-year Jewish rule.

Rome's 677 years (63 B.C.–A.D. 614) was the longest continuous occupation by any outside Great Power, and also the most constructive; and about 15 years ago, Rome's heir, Italy, did in fact advance serious claims to the colonial possessions of the ancient Roman Empire.

The Arabs are apt to identify their 447-year rule (A.D. 638-1085) with the Moslem regime which prevailed continuously from A.D. 638 to the present, and claim 1300 years. But this 1300-year span was Arab only in its first 447 years. Thereafter it was successively Seljuk, Mameluke, and Ottoman Turk. However, the position of the Arabs in Palestine is unique, for unlike all the other foreign conquerors, they did not hold themselves aloof but, instead, made Moslem converts of the natives, settled down as residents, and intermarried with them, with the result that all are now so completely Arabized that we cannot tell where the Canaanites leave off and the Arabs begin.

The present Hashemite Kingdom of Jordan claims to re-establish the right-to-rule once inaugurated by their Arab ancestors, just as the present Israel claims to re-establish the right-to-rule once inaugurated by their Hebrew ancestors; but the two of them exercise divided control of Palestine, and neither can be considered stable, for both are and have been from the first either in a state of war or of armistice pending final decision. Until that decision is made, the status of both cannot but be in question, and for this reason their brief nine-year terms have not been added to the ancestral rule but have been put in the short-and-divided category.

The Ottoman Turks of Turkey were the only recent Great Power long-termers, their 401-year rule beginning in 1517 and extending down into our own era to the end of World War I (1918).

The list now reads:

Conqueror	*Priority*	*Length of Rule–Years*	*Recent Rule*
Egypt	Yes	615	No
Jews	No	414	No
Roman Empire	No	677	No
Arabs	No	447	No
Turkey	No	401	Yes

If judged strictly on the grounds of one-time political possession by their ancestors (on which they base their political claims), *neither Arab Jordan nor Jewish Israel can qualify.* The records of both the Arabs and the Jews are outclassed by Egypt, the prior Great Power conqueror; Rome, whose rule was longest; and Turkey, which had recent possession. If conquest and dominion ever give validity, then the claims of Egypt, Rome, and Turkey are valid, if they wish to make such claims. (The fact revealed by these statistics—that Egypt actually has a better right in Palestine than Israel—is surely one of the most sardonic in all history.)

Judged on this historical record, *neither Jordan nor*

Israel has a shred of legal right in Palestine. Which makes their claims equally as, if not more, farcical than were the claims of Mussolini fifteen years ago to ancient Rome's colonial empire.

And so, failing to establish their right-through-inheritance, Israel and the Hashemite Kingdom of Jordan appear in their true status as invaders. Their names are merely the latest added to the long list of aggressors from without, for they, too, seized Palestine in the psychological moment of Great Power disruption following World War II. Their only right is of present possession—short-term and divided possession.

Who, then, has the legal right to Palestine?

There is one people, almost unmentioned, ignored, and practically forgotten. But they must be named and considered, for they are the most important of all—the native Palestinians themselves.

So far as history knows, they originated in the Canaanites who were the first occupants of the land, the original settlers. When any of the conquerors of the crossroads took prisoners in ancient times, they took them from the cities they besieged and captured. They did not take the time and trouble to go out into the remote valleys and ferret out the inhabitants one by one. So we may be sure that from the beginning, the settled population in the rural districts and small villages remained the same. We may be equally sure that the original stock—the ancient Canaanites—remained where they were, and their descendants did likewise.

It is true that they received an admixture of blood from each of the invaders, especially from the Egyptians, who were the rulers so often and so long. The Hyksos, the Hittites, and the Amorites, as well as the ancient

Assyrians and Babylonians must have added their quotas. There must be, even today, some heritage from the feather-crowned Philistines, who settled in such numbers as to give the land their name.

Because of the disapproval of mixed marriages, the ancient Israelites probably contributed little. But there was Persian blood, and Greek and Roman, no doubt, as well as Turk, both Seljuk and Ottoman.

Among today's people in Palestine, blue eyes are attributed to the Crusaders. And, of course, there is probably a higher percentage of Arab blood than any other, for the Arabs flooded the country, settled down, intermarried, and stayed.

But all these were additions, sprigs grafted onto the parent tree to mingle its sap with theirs. And that parent tree was Canaanite. The Canaanites were first. And when we speak of "Palestinians" or of the "Arab" population, we bear in mind their Canaanite origin.

This is important, for their legal right to the country today stems—not as the Arabs seem to think—from the long period of Arab rule, but from the fact that the Canaanites were first, which gives them *priority;* their descendents have continued to live there, which gives them *continuity;* and (except for the 800,000 dispossessed refugees) they are still living there, which gives them *present possession.* Thus we see that on purely statistical grounds they have a proven legal right to their own land.

Even granting that this were not true, the modern democratic world—through various declarations of principle, including the Atlantic Charter—has stated its belief in a right which transcends any sovereignty of conquest—the right of the people of any country to govern themselves. This, too, would give the Palestinians a right to their own self-government in their own country, Palestine.

But, as we have seen, the Palestinians have never in their long history been able to form a stable government for themselves; they did not have the time nor the opportunity, for they were a much-coveted crossroads and were always seized by some Great Power.

Even now, as always in the past, they are a subject people ruled by the two latest invaders—Israel and Jordan—which are now entrenched in Palestine, a *fait accompli.*

It is no good for us to wish the invaders Israel and Jordan were not there. They *are* there. They are in authority; they have the heady power to say yes and no to the greatest nations in the world and to the United Nations. This they know and take full advantage of, just as though they had a real right in Palestine and real power to implement their decisions.

But there is one angle neither of them has realized. In seizing Palestine and substituting themselves for the Palestinian population, they have subjected themselves to the same set of conditions which has throughout history made the Palestinians captives of outside Great Powers. Israel and Jordan have jointly taken over this role now, have substituted themselves for the Palestinians, have made themselves the scapegoat, the offering, and we can only hope they will not prove to be a burnt offering.

Let us repeat: *In taking over the crossroads, Israel and Jordan have put themselves in positions where, never in history, have the people been able to stay free.*

The present position of Israel and Jordan is, therefore, one of deadly danger at the crossroads, exposed as they are on all four sides to possible attack. Aliens, with only a toe hold, they now occupy a perilous traffic intersection which has never in its history been able to stay free of Great Power domination and, in case of world disruption, could not now stay free, least of all now. World civilization has progressed mightily, especially in the peaceful Western Hemisphere, but it has not yet worked itself out of its state of barbarism, of a tendency—particularly in the Old World—to seize and devour. That being the case, we may be pardonably realistic in estimating that present conditions at the crossroads, being an extension of those of the past, will continue along the same lines of Great Power struggle for some time to come, probably through the lifetime of Israel-Jordan, and possibly through the lifetimes of several of their successors.

The best weak and small Israel and Jordan can hope for is that the Great Powers, simulating righteousness, will stand back and keep hands off. This they may do so long as no world crisis explodes, and *providing Israel and Jordan themselves are well-behaved*

But if either begins to be a too dangerously active "trouble spot," then each of the Great Powers will perforce "protect its own interests." The quickest and most agile will grab the Palestine crossroads, and Israel and Jordan will be the perfect examples of the grass which in the morning groweth up and in the evening is cut down.

Some of Israel-Jordan's people may remain (as in the past), but their governments will inevitably disappear, as those of their short-term predecessors have disappeared, and, like them, will be seen no more, for neither of the two small, sporadic states is inherently strong enough to re-establish itself.

Their only hope of survival is to avoid any taint or connotation of "trouble spot" and to cooperate in at least maintaining local peace.

Do Israel and Jordan realize these frightening facts? We may venture the opinion that they do not, for their actions convey no indication of any such realization.

Instead we find Israel engaged in a program of conquest and expansion by aggression, of seizing sections of another country and boldly refusing to let them go.

While all the bordering Arab nations, for their part, arm for war.

The only solution to the whole situation seems to be for the United Nations to find some *new* plan which will not only be acceptable to both Israel and Jordan but may possibly insure their safety.

Because the Moslem philosophy is to acknowledge truths self-evident and attribute the necessity for life's readjustments to the will of God, the Arab nations may possibly accept any plan that affords a commendable and dignified way out of the presently insupportable position.

But the Israelis, preoccupied with their visions of a Restoration of the Kingdom of David and Solomon, may close their minds to the verdict rendered by history: (a) that they have no legal, political right in Palestine; and (b) even if they could gain the entire country, they could not maintain their own independence.

Israel will not give up easily, for it has one final argument: "Palestine may not be ours by political right. But we are entitled to it on spiritual grounds—it is the land God promised us and gave us. We have a spiritual right to it."

American Jews who were dubious about Israel's political right to Palestine are almost as convinced as the Israelis themselves that Israel has a spiritual right to the country, even to the whole of it, for they too know it is the Promised Land—the land God promised them.

As for Christians—this is the argument that makes them pause and reach for their Bibles and read the verses in which God promised the land to the Patriarch Abraham and his descendants.

Do the Jews have a *spiritual right* to Palestine?

This is the question, the last remaining question, but the most important one of all. It must be answered before the Palestine problem can be settled.

Spiritual Rights

AND SO AT LAST we come to the deciding evidence, the final criterion.

Contrary to our expectations, these religious factors will also prove definite and easy to grasp, for we have an almost visual example of them before our eyes as we read. It is Jerusalem, the city set on a hill.

At first glance few will accept Jerusalem as such an example. The modern Palestine tourist will exclaim incredulously, "What! Jerusalem spiritual! Why, it's the greediest and poorest-spirited, the most dilapidated and rotting and mildewed place we've ever seen!" It has been called a hotbed of suspicion and persecution; an ogre which has devoured the dead and cast their bones over the walls; cruel, intolerant, arrogant, furtive and secretive, terrifying, violent, cold with pride and hot with hate, a harridan, a slattern, a derelict, a beggar and a cesspool of intrigue. One of our greatest travel writers compares it to a tawny lion crouched menacingly on the hilltop "watchful, vindictive and ready to kill." External Jerusalem may be all these things now.

Certainly it has been in the past a locale of terrifying violence: twenty-two sieges and repeated destructions. It has been razed and pillaged; has been the volcanic setting for malevolent persecution, murder and crucifixion; and has been swept by tragic famine and virulent pestilence. All this we know and admit.

But, as we shall also see, Jerusalem epitomizes the entire religious record of the western world. In this one city originated and is continued the whole story of our spiritual progress from the beginning to the present. This story parallels the political history. Side by side, they run along together, mutually influencing each other, sometimes merging.

First, let us place Jerusalem in Biblical geography and identify it by its various names and pertinent titles: Genesis, Chapter 10, tells us that the lands belonging to Canaan (Ham's son and Noah's grandson) stretched between the ports of Sidon and Gaza on the Mediterranean and extended inland to Sodom and Gomorrah on the Dead Sea and produced many Canaanite settlements and cities, among which was the city of Jebus (whose inhabitants were naturally called Jebusites).

The Bible identifies the city of Jebus with Jerusalem—"Jebus which is Jerusalem" (Judges 19:10); "Jebusi which is Jerusalem" (Joshua 18:28).

There was something special about Jebus from history's very first mention of it in ancient Egyptian records when it was, as we know, a colonial possession, for it had a descriptive title, Uru-salem, which means City of Peace (Uru, city of, and Salem, peace), a title which evolved early into the now familiar Jerusalem. Genesis 14:18 also uses the name, City of Salem or City of Peace. Thus its special character was established from our first Biblical as well as historical knowledge of it.

But in what way was the city connected with God?

For man's first dealings with God we go back as far as

we can into antiquity. Authorities on religions tell us that primitive peoples, no matter how numerous their local beneficent and malevolent minor gods, also have a conception, perhaps dim and vague and shadowy, of one supreme deity, paramount and infinitely higher than all the others, a "most high God."

Eventually the dim and shadowy presentiment of this supreme power emerged in man's mind and throughout the ages has developed into the clear concept of God the Father and Creator in Whom we moderns now believe.

But when and where was God first realized with sufficient clarity and awareness to prompt priests to minister to Him in organized worship? Theologians indulge in vast speculation: Did Abraham discover God in Ur? Or did Moses discover him in Sinai?

A painstaking search of the Bible reveals the fact that *Jerusalem* is the first place named as the seat of priestly worship of the Most High God and that a *Canaanite* is the first man named as a priest of God: "Melchizedek, King of Salem—he was the priest of the most high God" (Genesis 14:18).

Did God choose Jerusalem because it was already a city of peace, or did it attain that character after His worship was set up there?

And why was Jerusalem the geographical spot chosen for God and peace? A rather logical answer, or at least a possible one suggests itself, that the realization of God may have been a natural outgrowth of the worship of some lesser deity, a local god whose abode was a rock or a tree or a spring in the vicinity. For Jerusalem had such an abode in the Rock Moriah.

Today this great rock, even to the modern scientific mind, is puzzling and disquieting. Although the Temple

Area in Jerusalem is the leveled top of a cream-colored limestone ridge, the Rock Moriah is glistening black, a great alien boulder as big as a house lying half buried in the west center of the Temple Area, in the gloom of the huge rotunda of the Moslem mosque called the Dome of the Rock which is built over it.

A protective lattice-work fence encloses the rock to baffle vandal tourists who would like nothing better than to chip it away piecemeal for souvenirs. But in one spot the lattice slats have become loosened and can be pushed aside.

By reaching in at arm's length, a palm can be laid on "the rock." It is a startling, almost a frightening experience because it is a surprise—one jerks one's hand away. In some peculiar way, the rock is alive, and lets you know it, for it communicates—certainly not an electric shock—but a vitality equally definite though less definable. The Rock Moriah seems as full of power as though it had from the creation of the world stored up energy, perhaps absorbed as on a perpetual photographic plate the procession of great events which had transpired there; and like a phonograph disc had recorded all the sounds, the ancient rituals and blessings down through the ages, and is throbbing silently with them and almost ready to hum. One has the extra-sensory realization that the Rock Moriah wants to speak and say something that it feels should be said.

If today this great boulder can thus shock the informed mind, what must have been its impact in primitive times? To the Ancients, who were chronologically nearer than we to the source-of-things, whose ears, like a dog's, were capable of distinguishing sounds our ears can't hear now, it must have been an object of terrifying power whose voice was actually audible at times and whose authority and control could easily grow and spread from local to universal proportions as the god-of-the-rock manifested greater and greater power and grew and changed into an entirely new concept—the Supreme God of the Universe.

Whatever the circumstances of its development, the concept of a Supreme or "most high" God was already clear in men's minds and the seat of his worship was already established by the Canaanites in Jebus, the City of Peace, before the Patriarch Abram's arrival there. For when he, a sojourner in the Land of Canaan, rescued his nephew Lot and other locals from foreign raiders and returned triumphant, "Melchizedek, king of Salem, brought forth bread and wine; and he was the priest of the most high God. And he blessed him and said, Blessed be Abram of the most high God, possessor of heaven and earth" (Genesis 14:18, 19). Let us note this last phrase, "possessor of heaven and earth," for it indicates the ultimate in supremacy. Thus *Abram was blessed by the most high God of the City of Peace*. He had received the Blessing.

Lest there be any question that this was the God who became the God of Abram, let us also note that immediately following the blessing, Abram swore by this God, *now his patron,* took a solemn oath, referring to Him in the same words as those used by Melchizedek: "I have lift up mine hand unto the Lord, the most high God, the possessor of heaven and earth" (Genesis 14:22).

In the next chapter, in the very next breath so to speak, the ancient chronicler of this section of Genesis tells of Abram's prayer, "Lord God, what wilt thou give me?" (Genesis 15:2) and God's promise, "In the same day the

Lord made a covenant with Abram saying, Unto thy seed have I given this land" (Genesis 15:18).

It was as simple as that. The highest power in Canaan, the Supreme Deity "possessor of heaven and earth" which certainly included Canaan, had promised the Land of Canaan to Abram.

Who was this Abram, where had he come from and how did he, a sojourner and newcomer, fit into the picture?

The fascinating thought occurs that he may have been a distant cousin of Melchizedek, the man who blessed him. The Bible says that Canaan, the original settler in the country, begot the Jebusites (I Chronicles 1:14). Melchizedek was king of the city-state of Jebus, so it is logical that he was a scion of the reigning house and therefore a descendant of its founder, Canaan. If so, Melchizedek and Abram were cousins many times removed, for their ancestral lines had begun side by side in two of Noah's sons, Ham and Shem. Ham fathered Canaan who settled in the Land of Canaan, while Shem fathered Arphaxad who settled, it is thought, across Arabia at the head of the Persian Gulf where his descendants continued to live for eight generations to the time of Abram who then migrated west across Arabia to the Land of Canaan.

In the old days, following the Flood, when Noah's family was still together, Canaan had sinned and Grandfather Noah had decreed his punishment—that Canaan should be the servant to Shem. Perhaps Melchizedek, in giving Shem's scion Abram the Land of Canaan and the blessing of the Most High God, was merely fulfilling a recognized obligation and executing Noah's decree.

But there was an obstacle—Abram and his wife Sarah were childless and had no sons to inherit the land and the blessing. When they were both aged and hope for children seemed gone Abram took another wife, Hagar, who bore him a son, Ishmael.

The Arabs, who are descendants of this first-born son Ishmael, make a great point of the fact that Hagar, though a bondwoman, was *not* a concubine, but is designated in the Bible as Abram's wife. Sarah "gave her to her husband Abram to be his wife" (Genesis 16:3). That Hagar should have been made a wife was also logical, for she was the woman by whom Abram hoped to father an undisputed heir to the land and the blessing.

But when Abram was a hundred years old a second son, Isaac, was born to him and his first wife, Sarah, so Abram had not one son but two.

In gratitude to the Supreme Deity who had blessed him and given him so much, Abraham determined to give God a gift in return, the best he could offer, his dearest possession, his younger son Isaac, whom he would sacrifice as a burnt offering. And where should he go to present this gift but to the place where God was?

Leaving Beersheba, Abram went into the land of Moriah and Jewish tradition says that he built an altar on Mount Moriah, perhaps in the very spot where he had received God's blessing, possibly on the great and mysterious Rock itself, and laid the wood on it, and bound his son Isaac and laid him on the altar and took the fire in his hand to kindle the wood.

At this tense moment the angel of the Lord called to him and when Abraham looked up he saw a ram, a substitute offering, caught in a thicket. With infinite gratitude, for he realized anew that God was safeguarding him and his family, Abram released his son Isaac and sacrificed the ram, and it was with this younger son Isaac that God renewed his covenant.

Family friction finally forced Abram (now called Abraham) to set Hagar and the elder son Ishmael out in the desert. There they not only survived but flourished for God blessed Ishmael (Genesis 17:20) and fulfilled his repeated promise to Abraham to make Ishmael a great people.

Isaac, at home, was his father's heir—heir to the promise of Canaan. That promise was long in fulfillment. Abraham and Isaac died. Their offspring, now called Israelites, migrating to Egypt, were enslaved there, and escaped at long last when Moses led their famed Exodus, then wandered forty years in the desert where Moses, too, died.

Then under Joshua the Israelites invaded the Land of Canaan but failed to conquer it, and "dwelt among the Canaanites, Hittites, Amorites, and Perizzites and Hivites and Jebusites," (Judges 3:5) where they were again repeatedly in bondage, to Jabin King of Canaan, to Midian, to the Philistines.

It was not until they organized themselves under a king of their own that they were able to hold their own. David, their second king and a soldier-poet, conquered Canaan as we know about 1000 B.C., made it an independent Israelite kingdom and thus was God's promise to Abraham fulfilled. *At long last the Promise was fulfilled.* And David's capital was Jerusalem where God had blessed Abraham.

But the king had displeased God and as a result the Israelites were being decimated by pestilence. David and his elders gathered to repent in sackcloth. Where did they go for this ceremony? Naturally, to the strangely vital Rock Moriah, where David was petrified to see an angel with a drawn sword.

This rock was still the property of the Jebusite (Canaanite) kings and was used as a threshing floor, perhaps a ceremonial threshing floor for the first fruits of the grain. Araunah, the current king, offered the rock and its threshing equipment to David: "All these things did Araunah as a king, give to the king" (II Samuel 24:23).

David bought the Rock Moriah and, as God commanded, built there an altar where his progenitor Abraham had built one ages before. Later, David's son Solomon built a beautiful temple on the same spot and it is believed that Solomon's altar before the Temple was placed over the rock.

Although the Promise was now fulfilled, its first and last chapters enacted here, this is not the last time the Rock appears in the story of man's spiritual progress. On the contrary it appears again and again through the ages and becomes increasingly important with each appearance.

But following Solomon's accession to the throne it suffered an evil fate for instead of preserving there the purity of worship of the Most High God, the Israelites debased it, so the Bible states. Solomon himself was guilty of idolatry and at his death his newly-founded kingdom fell apart.

Instead of forsaking their transgressions the two halves of the kingdom, or rather the two resultant kingdoms, Israel and Judah, continued to sin, indulging in all manner of vice and paganism which flourished—from the Baal-incense burned daily on the flat rooftops to the child-consuming fires of Moloch in the Valley of Hinnom. The creeping evil finally flooded into the Temple and manifested itself in secret wicked rites—this on the very spot where Abraham had heard the words of God and where David had seen the avenging angel with sword outstretched over Jerusalem.

Thundering voices of successive prophets warned of doom and the twin kingdoms diminished in proportion as the vice increased. God had warned Solomon: "I will cut off Israel out of the land which I have given them" (I Kings 9:7). "I will surely rend the kingdom from thee and give it to thy servants" (I Kings 11:11). We must admit that these were promises too.

The later prophets warned with equal vehemence, but to no avail. In 722 B.C. Assyria conquered the northern kingdom of Israel and carried its inhabitants away into captivity, and in 586 B.C. the same fate befell Judah when Babylon conquered her and carried her people away.

And thus was the Promised Land lost. The Promise, which had been fulfilled amid such rejoicing was lost amid lamentation.

There was one redeeming feature however—although the northern kingdom of Israel disintegrated permanently, God's prophets gave Judah reassurance, "I will have mercy upon the house of Judah and will save them by the Lord their God."

This promise of mercy and salvation was fulfilled when Persia conquered Babylon and permitted the Babylonian captives to return and rebuild their temple in Jerusalem and reestablish the worship of God there. But it was a spiritual restoration only and not a temporal one,— "and will not save them by the bow nor by the sword, nor by battle," (Hosea 1:7) for the province of Judah did not gain independence, but was part of the Persian Empire and remained under Persian rule.

The Israelites, now called Jews because the people of Judah were the last surviving remnant of the race, had freedom of worship in Jerusalem even though they had irrevocably lost political possession of the Promised Land which passed through succeeding centuries from Persian to Greek to Roman.

These Romans were to be the rulers of the land during the next great step in its spiritual development. At first they governed the Jews through a vassal king, Herod, who rebuilt the Temple on Mount Moriah for them, on the site of the great Rock, a temple larger in size and richer in appointments than its predecessors, richer even than the Temple of Solomon had been. Scattered Jews from all parts of the world came, in pilgrimage, bringing rich gifts and here once again was given to the Jews the opportunity to make permanent the establishment of a pure worship of the Most High God.

Instead, material interests predominated and the worship became commercialized. Temple tithe collectors, more adept at the shakedown than modern racketeers, had their rival mobs fighting each other in the streets like gangsters; and the money changers with their tables set up in the Temple itself acted as middlemen for the high priests and extorted money mercilessly from the helpless pilgrims.

And so the stage was set for the next and what we of the western world believe was the greatest step in the advancement of religion. This movement, an intended reformation, was led by Jesus of Nazareth, a descendant of the ancient King David who had conquered Jerusalem a thousand years earlier.

Never before had God brought forth a spokesman who saw so clearly as did Jesus of Nazareth the possibility that all the children of God the Father, from the lowest to the highest, could be united in a brotherhood of peace.

But such a peaceful brotherhood presupposes goodness, and when Jesus came to Jerusalem, to the temple on the site of the Rock, as to a magnet, he was as horrified by the wickedness he found there as the prophets of old had been by the evils they denounced so vigorously.

But he was a physically braver man than those early prophets who had warred only verbally on wickedness for he illustrated his words by strong, direct action—"and Jesus went into the temple and began to cast out them that sold and bought in the temple and overthrew the tables of the money-changers, and the seats of them that sold doves; and would not suffer that any man should carry any vessel through the temple, and he taught, saying unto them, Is it not written, My house shall be called of all nations the house of prayer? but ye have made it a *den of thieves*" (St. Mark 11:15-17).

Of course the outraged Jewish priesthood immediately sentenced Jesus to death, a sentence carried out by the Roman police force.

But before Jesus died he foretold the doom, not of the political kingdom of the Jews, for that was already lost, but the extinction of their religious center, the Temple: "Seest thou these great buildings? there shall not be left one stone upon another that shall not be thrown down" (St. Mark 13:2).

Not only was the prophecy of destruction of the temple fulfilled a short forty years later, but in A.D. 135 the whole of Jerusalem was destroyed by the Romans, every Jew was expelled, an entirely new Roman city named Aelia Capitolina was built on the site, and all Jews were forbidden to enter it on penalty of death.

The Roman Empire lived in Palestine for over 600 years, but Caesars die, and others reign, and edicts change, and the Jews trickled back into Jerusalem, drawn by the conviction that this site was holy, and established unobtrusive synagogues among the many pagan Roman temples with their numerous gods. Here too came the followers of Jesus by the thousands, Christians brought by an equally strong conviction that the temple site where Jesus had taught, the streets he had walked with the cross, had been hallowed by his presence.

This multiplicity of religions existed everywhere, even to the remote Roman outpost cities eastward along the edges of the great Arabian desert, and word of them spread into the desert, to the ears of an Arab, one Mohammed. And thus was set in motion the next great religious movement, or rather the third and latest chapter in the history of the Most High God.

Who was this Mohammed? Oddly enough, he too was a relative of the Jews, for he was also a direct descendant of the Patriarch Abraham through his first-born son Ishmael whom the Most High God of Jerusalem had blessed.

To go back to the beginning of this neglected branch of the family: When Ishmael was a child, he and his mother had been set out in the desert, but had been watched over and in accordance with God's blessing had become a great nation—"And as for Ishmael, I have heard thee: Behold I have blessed him, and will make him fruitful and will multiply him exceedingly; twelve princes shall he beget, and I will make him a great nation" (Genesis 17:20).

As the angel of the Lord had foretold (Genesis 16:10) Ishmael's seed could not be numbered for multitude. Now, in the 7th century A.D., they were called Arabs and in uncounted thousands they filled the 1500-mile-long Peninsula of Arabia—and Mohammed was one of them.

He had been born in A.D. 570 in Mecca, an ancient shrine city midway down the west coast of the Peninsula. At that spot Abraham was believed to have built the shrine for a stone brought to him from heaven by the Angel Gabriel; and Hagar and Ishmael were believed to be buried there.

So Mohammed was conscious of his heritage, and he reminded his fellow Arabs of theirs'—their forefather Abraham's God.

Mohammed realized with mounting indignation that God now seemed demoted to the position of one among many and he became God's prophet, calling for a return to the realization of a Supreme Deity, the one, the original, the only God, the "God of Abraham," reiterating endlessly, "There is no God but God."

Thoughts which Mohammed believed to be revelations directly from God came into his mind. Compiled in written form they became the Koran, the authority for this renewed belief in one Supreme Deity and one only, called Allah in the Arabic language, just as He is called *Gott* in the German, and *Dieu* in the French.

It was a powerful renewal, too potent and strong to be

contained by the desert. It burst its bounds in sweeping attack against those whom Mohammed considered guilty of abandoning and betraying the Supreme Deity.

Who were these guilty of such betrayal? In Mohammed's view, the first and foremost were the Jews.

Mohammed fully realized God's great gift to Abraham, the ancestor of both the Arabs and the Jews: "We formerly gave unto the family of Abraham a book of revelation and wisdom; and we gave them a great kingdom" (*The Koran*, Ch. 4). He did not question that God had chosen the Jews, did not question that God had chosen Abraham's second son Isaac, the ancestor of the Jews, rather than his first-born Ishmael, who was the Arabs' own ancestor. Those were facts, matters of record.

What Mohammed did maintain was that the Jews had betrayed their trust: "God hath cursed them with their infidelity—for a vile price have they sold their souls" (*The Koran*, Ch. 2). Chosen, they had failed, a betrayal beyond dispute for they were convicted out of the mouths of their own prophets. They were convicted by the evidence of events too, for they had failed in their custodianship of the Promised Land by losing it. As a result, the entire Middle East including Jerusalem, the city where Abraham himself had been blessed, now teemed with alien beliefs.

Who could be better qualified to right this great wrong than the next of kin, those other descendants of Abraham who had remained true to Abraham's God—in other words, the Arabs themselves?

And, according to Mohammed, there was another wrong of which the Jews were guilty and for which they deserved punishment—they had "slain Christ Jesus the son of Mary, the apostle of God" (Ch. 4). Jesus was accepted as one of God's prophets, like Mohammed himself. "Verily Christ Jesus the son of Mary is the apostle of God" (Ch. 4).

However, the Christian followers of Jesus came in for their share of Mohammed's condemnation, for he believed they had departed from Jesus' teachings: "They are surely infidels who say, Verily God is Christ the son of Mary; since Christ said, O children of Israel serve God, my Lord and your Lord" (Ch. 5). And the idea of the divinity of Jesus was shocking to Mohammed, "They say, God hath begotten children: God forbid" (Ch. 2).

Mohammed believed that the pagan idolatry of the many Roman and Greek and local gods should also be wiped out. "We follow the religion of Abraham the orthodox who was no idolator" (Ch. 2).

He condemned the worship, so prevalent in some sections of the Middle East, of heavenly bodies. "Worship not the sun, neither the moon, but worship God who hath created them" (Ch. 41).

Mohammed recognized God's many apostles and prophets: "We believe in God, and that which hath been sent down unto us, and that which hath been sent down unto Abraham, and Ishmael, and Isaac, and Jacob, and the tribes, and that which was delivered unto Moses, and Jesus, and that which was delivered unto the prophets from their Lord. We make no distinction between any of them" (Ch. 2). Among these prophets he included himself. "There is no God but God, and Mohammed is His Prophet."

But, in accordance with this belief that there is no God but God, he drew a sharp line between the apostles, himself included, and God. There were to be no supplemental sharers in what was solely God's due: "It is not fit for a man that God should give him a book of revelations and wisdom, and prophecy, and then he should say unto men, Be ye worshipers of me besides God" (Ch. 3).

All these trespassers on God's glory, these would-be sharers in God's supremacy—the Jewish priesthood with their scrolls and worship of ritual, the Christians with their ikons and many saints, the Roman and Greek and Syrian idolators, and the Middle East sun-and-moon worshipers, Mohammed lumped together under the head of "Infidels" and without delay ordered their punishment. He declared a Holy War and told his followers (who called themselves Moslems and their religious world Islam), "War is enjoined you against the infidels" (Ch. 2).

The Arabs needed no second bidding. They came out of the desert in uncounted thousands and with the fiery zeal encountered only in those intent on wiping out evil, they conquered the whole of the Middle East.

Good Moslems believe that Mohammed himself came to Jerusalem and from the Rock Moriah ascended on his white war horse, Barak, to heaven. It is an arresting thought: perhaps it occurred on a brilliant moon-lit night with this old fighter-for-God sitting on his steed and rising triumphantly toward the stars, an incandescently white tableau against the blue darkness of the night sky.

The Arabs took Jerusalem, reestablished God's worship there, and have carried it on continuously for 1300 years up to and including the present. The poorest pilgrim can go to the Dome of the Rock and worship there as freely as the king himself.

To the Arabs, Jerusalem is a holy city—their progenitor Abraham was blessed there, Mohammed ascended thence to heaven, and it is from Jerusalem that Moslems will be resurrected on the Day of Judgment when they are judged by their ability to walk a horsehair (Mohammed holding one end, Jesus the other) which will stretch from the Mount of Olives across the Kedron Valley to the Dome of the Rock—the Rock.

The western world accords little importance to the religion of Mohammed. Let it not be minimized. To the devout Moslem, Mohammed's ascent to heaven is as real as Moses' reception of the Ten Commandments on Mount Sinai is to the Jew, or the birth of Jesus in a manger is to the Christian. But more important, this religion was the direct instrument which finally eradicated sun and moon worship in that part of the world where it was so deeply rooted. It also freed the Middle East so completely and finally from the last vestiges of idol worship that Moslems are still horrified at the thought of idols of any kind—they worship God only. This is now the religion of millions. The most ignorant of them will tell you with complete conviction that it is the only pure worship of God, for it has no trappings of any kind and is the only religion that has not been commercialized.

When prayer time comes, the good Moslem wherever he may be, in the field or beside the road, kneels and without adjuncts of any kind, prays. He faces toward Mecca, the place where Abraham built the shrine, but he prays to God and to God alone.

These Arabs then are the people who today stand on the east side of the armistice line in Palestine. They face, across the line to the west, the Jews, the people whom they consider the betrayers of God.

Israel on the other hand, considers its claim as based on the Promise to be indisputable, and demands an extended Israel (including the Negev, Edom, Moab, Ammon and Gilead) equal to that of the Kingdom of David and Solomon which was the fulfillment of the Promise. But the Kingdom of David and Solomon lasted for only 73 years, as we have seen. This would put it in the short-term class, which would invalidate it.

The actual Land of the Promise extended only from Dan to Beersheba in length and from the Jordan to the Mediterranean in width. When Moses led the ancient Israelites up to Kadesh-Barnea he was in the Negev and still outside the Promised Land for he sent men across the border to "spy out the country." And when Moses had led his followers round to the eastern border and stood on the heights beyond Jordan they were still outside the Promised Land, into which Moses was forbidden to enter. So there is no question about Moab, Ammon and Gilead—neither they nor the Negev were included in the Promise. So, if modern Israel is consistent, she should give up the Negev and her settlements east of Lake Huleh and the Sea of Galilee and withdraw inside the borders of the Promised Land.

But what about the validity of the Promise as applied to Palestine proper, within its recognized bounds from Dan to Beersheba and from the Jordan to the Mediterranean?

In that area, certainly the Promise provided the most valid of claims.

But the one great fact overlooked by modern Israel is that *that Promise was fulfilled.* It was fulfilled long ago, more than fulfilled, for as we have seen the ancient Kingdom of David and Solomon included more territory than the Promise included.

The other fact even more important is this: *The Prom-*

ise was lost. It was gained, then lost, finished, done, all in ancient times.

Once the Jews began to intrigue with outside Great Powers, that loss was inevitable, which should point a moral to modern Israel. When an outside power is appealed to for protection, it must perforce move in to establish that protection. Thus the small state loses its dearest possession—liberty—and loses it not to the enemy but to the friend, as Eastern Palestine has also lost its liberty to the friendly protector, the Hashemite Kingdom of Jordan, and as modern Israel will lose its liberty to the first foreign power that moves in to protect it.

When the ancient Babylonians conquered Judah, the last remaining remnant of the Jewish kingdom, its political existence as a state ended forever. The Jewish return to Jerusalem and the rebuilding of their temple under Ezra and Nehemiah was carried out not by a free people but by people who were subjects of Persia. It was a spiritual restoration only, not a political one (moral number two).

That spiritual restoration gained by men of rectitude and demonstrated in the rebuilding of the temple was jeopardized repeatedly in succeeding generations by the Jewish wars and was finally destroyed completely with the destruction of the Temple in A.D. 70 and the Dispersion in A.D. 135 (moral number three).

So we know that in ancient times *the Promise was fulfilled. And lost.* Any modern claim based on that Promise is not valid for it was a contract fulfilled and finished long ago.

If we apply the method of comparison used in the historical section, we must admit the religious position of the Arabs is the better one. They amalgamated with and in a way became the spiritual heirs of the native Canaanites who had been the first people we know to set up priestly worship of the Supreme Deity, which gives them *priority*. For 1300 years the Moslems have faithfully guarded the Holy City of Jerusalem, a record for continuity unsurpassed by any other of God's followers. And the Moslems have *present possession.*

In the present crisis the modern Arab feels that the Jew, to put it in the vernacular, hasn't a leg to stand on. Chosen by God, he abandoned God and followed after strange gods, and through venality lost the Holy Land.

After its first loss, God promised and gave the Jews a second opportunity to restore their spiritual center at Jerusalem but this was also lost, and the Jews were then absent from Palestine for 1800 years.

Notwithstanding this long absense, and although God had *not* promised another restoration after the Roman dispersion, the modern Jews by various means invaded Palestine, set up the state of Israel, and have recently attempted the capture of Jerusalem itself. Arabs living in Jerusalem will tell you seriously that God protected the walled city and kept it from the Jews.

On the other hand, the Arabs feel that their own position is unassailable. Originally discriminated against, they are the only people faithful to God. They rescued the Holy City, have cherished and protected it for 1300 years and have not the slightest intention of yielding this center of God's worship to the very people whom they consider to have desecrated it, and been repeatedly unfaithful to God in the past.

Whether we like it or not, this is the Arab position. To them it is incomprehensible that we of the western world can see any justice whatever in the claims of the Jews. The Arabs themselves see the whole situation so plainly, their own rightness, and the Jews' wrongness—why can't the western world see it? And particularly why can't Americans, the champions of right, the condemners of wrong, see it? Why do they go on supporting the Jews and even occasionally voicing the fantastic opinion that the Jews of all people should be given Jerusalem?

Until we Americans grasp this Arab viewpoint, their deep religious conviction of the Jews' wrongdoing, we can have no real understanding of that which divides the two races. When we do understand, we see that this past religious history is the real cause of the division. It is of such magnitude that it is as though the armistice line, the political hair line crack between Israel and Jordan, had become as wide and unbridgeable as the ocean.

For, across on the other side, stand the Jews. The Promise, once lost, has *not* been renewed, but they ignore that. With the animosity of the loser dedicated to recovery they face the Arabs and inch forward wherever they see a weakness in the line, determined that now once again, this time with all their own tremendous wealth to help them, and world sympathy to support them, they will retake Jerusalem, the religious center which they possessed three thousand years ago.

Can the wide abyss between the two races ever be wiped out, eradicated? With these implacable, age-old enemies facing each other as belligerents can their differences ever be compromised and peace brought to the Middle East? How can any UN Commission ever solve this problem? How can any peace treaty ever be written? Where begin?

And we cannot ignore the Christian religion. The Christian world makes no temporal claims of any kind but Jesus taught here, originated the beliefs now held by our entire western world, here gave his life rather than retract those beliefs. Whatever the western world has of constructive Christianity—active kindliness, feeding the poor, rescuing the unfortunate, caring for the sick (and Christian nations do more in that respect than all the remainder of the world together)—is the direct outgrowth of Jesus' teaching that every man, "even the least," is our brother.

Of the three faiths represented in Jerusalem today, Christianity is by far the most vital, for it carries on these good works there. Although the city is in the hands of the Moslems, it is the home of countless active Christian institutions: St. George's Anglican Church and Orphanage, the Lutheran Church of the Redeemer and Headquarters of the Lutheran Middle East Federation, St. Anne's Church, Franciscan Biblical Institute and Library, Sisters of Zion Convent, Spanish Sisters of Calvary School, St. Catherine Church, Franciscan Orphan Girls School, St. Michael Church, St. Sidnya Church, St. Saviour Church, Franciscan Orphan Boys School, St. Vasilios Church, Collège des Frères, St. Theodosi Church, St. Nicola Church, Greek Orthodox Patriarchate, Latin Patriarchate, St. Mitri School, Church of the Holy Sepulchre, Church of All Nations, Russian Orthodox Church, Carmelite Convent, Church of the Lord's Prayer, St. Stephen's Church and Dominican Fathers Library, Benedictine Monastery, St. James Cathedral, St. Abraham Monastery, Greek Catholic Patriarchate, St. Joseph's Girls School, Maronite Convent, Syrian Orthodox Monastery, Armenian Orthodox Monastery and Library,

Armenian Orthodox Patriarchate, Christ Church, and many more.

Relations between Moslems and Christians are most cordial. It is told of the late King Abdullah of Trans-Jordan, who came from Amman to Jerusalem every Friday to worship at the Dome of the Rock, that he and Dr. Moll, the head of the Lutheran Federation, stood together one day looking out the window at a long Lutheran caravan setting out to bring great bales of reconditioned clothing to an Arab refugee camp. The King turned to Dr. Moll and remarked, "That is the kind of religion I can understand."

And so this is the religious past and present of Jebus, Urusalem, the city of Salem, the city of Peace, Jerusalem. The change of name from Urusalem to Jerusalem was a change of more than mere vowels and consonants, for it was symbolic of the tragic change wrought by the many conquerors who came, after Melchizedek, and debased the city.

But before and throughout all this degradation, some peculiar internal quality in Jerusalem continued to draw the world's greatest spiritual leaders and make this one spot the setting for the greatest steps forward the world has known. This internal quality must have been very great in the past and can still be felt by anyone who remains in Jerusalem for any length of time. If the visitor searches for a visible symbol of it, neither the Wailing Wall nor the controversial Church of the Holy Sepulchre nor yet the Dome of the Rock will fulfill his expectance, but perhaps the Rock Moriah will, for in it is condensed the history of the three.

Rock is rock and not spirit, but anyone who knows the Rock Moriah's tremendous history—majestic, tragic, sublime—knows that this is inherently a special place on the earth's surface, otherwise why have all these great events transpired here?

When, and by what means, was Jerusalem first singled out?

Did God simply choose it in the beginning and give it His blessing? Even in Melchizedek's time it was known as the City of Peace, perhaps because it was the worship center of the Most High God. Was this worship old and well established in Melchizedek's era? Had it begun far back in the early dawn of time? Or had it been established by the Canaanite Melchizedek himself, a man so famous as God's priest that even the scribes of another race recognized his position and recorded his name for posterity? We know only that he, a *Canaanite,* was the *first known priest* of God and that Jerusalem was the first known site of God's organized worship. (Perhaps we are indebted to the Canaanites not only for our alphabet but for our knowledge of God.)

Even if Melchizedek were the original discoverer of God, he must have had some good reason for establishing worship in Jerusalem. Perhaps the City of Peace had in some way earned this accolade. It may be that in some bygone age some deed of profound greatness had released a spiritual essence which consecrated it and permeated forever its rocks and stones. Each great even in succeeding ages may have added, has undoubtedly added, to its sacred stature.

Because God chose Jerusalem as the seed-plot, the germinating point of our spiritual growth, and the continuing field down through the ages of mankind's increasing harvest we cannot escape the realization that this ground was from the beginning and, regardless of present externals, still is, hallowed, if not inherently, then by these events. We realize at last that Jerusalem is a great and holy city.

And we have the odd feeling that Jerusalem knows it, too. Sentient with the awareness often informing inanimate matter, the very rocks and stones seem to say, "Put off thy shoes from off thy feet, for the place whereon thou standest is holy ground!"

Feeling these things, the modern visitor to Jerusalem sees its physical deterioration as a tragedy, as though some great man, still with greatness in his soul, had been beaten and abused and kicked about until he became a physical wreck. Jerusalem has suffered every imaginable indignity and insult and degradation, has been battered and beaten too, razed and destroyed again and again. Pestilence, murder, crucifixion, famine, even cannibalism, have desecrated it. It is not alone that Jesus was crucified here. So has Jerusalem been crucified, time and again. Not one street, but every street in the city is a Via Dolorosa.

And why? Because religious powers even more than temporal powers have fought for it. And the magnificent irony is that the three warring religions all worship the same God!

Surely, surely, this points to the answer, the only solution of the problem, makes it crystal clear. This holy site should be above all religions and sacred only to God.

To belong to any one single race or nation or religion has not been the way to peace in the past and therefore is not the way to peace now. The city does not morally belong to any *one*. And Jerusalem will not be captive to any one but will be the scene of dissension so long as any one power, either religious or temporal, tries to impose captivity.

If the Rock Moriah, bursting with its stored knowledge, could speak, what would it say? This? "Here on this spot which God chose, here where man first knelt to God, let all the world come freely! Come in amity, as brothers, making this again a City of Peace!"

Jerusalem's ideal destiny the fitting outcome of its magnificent religious history is that of a universal monument to God, free to all followers of God. The UN itself has officially recognized the unique character of Jerusalem as a Holy City.

But what of Palestine, the country as a whole? That is the present problem. It is important, for it endangers world peace.

Is military force the answer? No. That is the quickest way to war. And besides, there is no military force either inside or outside Palestine strong enough to protect Israel and Jordan from extinction should the Great Powers decide to intervene. And some of them only await a pretext. Force cannot stop them, for they are the stronger.

The only plan of the United Nations was a proposed Trusteeship to be administered locally by a governor appointed by the United Nations. Which takes us back precisely to the days of Jerusalem under a British Mandate from the League of Nations, whose results we know too well!

No, let us depart once and for all from the rut of "Trusteeship" thinking. The term has too many connotations of potential violence under static control.

And although the great modern democracies have set

up one perfect, idealistic goal—eventual independent self-rule for every nation in the world, whether great or small—independence is not the answer in this case. If all nations were equally important this goal could ultimately be achieved. But Palestine is a *special* spot, a *crossroads.* And let us recognize the facts of life: Independent states there have never throughout the whole of history been able to stay free and, present world conditions being an extension of those in the past, cannot now stay free. Israel and Jordan are at present independent, but their problem is not solved. Continuation along this line is futile.

We can only conclude that as a special spot Palestine requires a special status and a wider protection. We must offer a radically new and different approach.

But Israel and Jordan have the power of yes and no, and they are irreconcilable. What then is to be done? If Israel will not change, if Jordan will not change, then one thing remains: conditions must change. Actually, conditions must *be* changed. How can this be accomplished?

The first requisite is to alter our own thinking, to get completely away from the only two solutions now known—either trusteeship, or independence after a peace treaty for both nations.

"Trusteeship" with its connotation of immaturity within and domination from without would be a humiliating and niggardly answer, a step backward into feudalism. Even the word is a hated word and a trouble breeder, automatically initiating ugly patterns of thought and violent reflexes, so trusteeship is not to be considered.

The independence which would seem assured after a

peace treaty will prove in a world crisis to be the quickest road to extinction.

But what else is there? Our task is to find and sell Jordan and Israel a new and attractive solution. It must be good, better than what they have now; otherwise they will say no.

Actually, what each has now is pitifully little, if he will only stop whistling in the dark long enough to admit it. Neither can keep order, both are desperate for money, neither could survive in a world crisis, but both would be gobbled up and eradicated. So, if we were niggardly bargainers we would not have to offer much.

But we are not niggardly bargainers. We would be ashamed to offer something small and mean. The modern world has a keen sense of the worth and dignity of man and we feel that the best is none too good for the people of Palestine, both Jews and Arab-Canaanites, who have probably suffered more throughout history than those of any other spot in the world. Any plan offered must be based on lofty idealism, an ethical step upward, something progressive, a plan which will bring a sparkle of pleasure to the eye and hope to the heart, a plan which will restore confidence in the goodness of God and of man.

The only remaining possibility is the setting up of some moral barrier strong enough to serve as a fence, such as that moral barrier which now protects the Vatican.

But the moral barrier protecting the Vatican is created, not by any outside elements but by the character of that institution itself.

Therefore: a moral barrier for Palestine can only be created, not by anything done on the outside but by a change in the character of Palestine itself, only by raising it to such a superior status that public opinion will recognize it as inviolate, and not permit any breaking of that taboo.

How can this be done?

First of all, what is Palestine's character now? What do we have to work with?

We know, how well we know, that Palestine is now and has been for thousands of years a trampled crossroads, a political pawn, traded, invaded, a subject people, sometimes a vassal, or a protectorate, or a satellite, or a mandate, annexed, dismembered, devastated, denuded, burned, partitioned.

But perhaps this is not its character. Perhaps these are only external scars, inflicted by multiple outside injuries. Let us look beneath this battered surface.

The United Nations 1947, *Report on Palestine,* has this to say on page 146: "(a) Palestine, as the Holy Land, occupies a unique position in the world. It is sacred to Christian, Jew and Moslem alike. The spiritual interests of hundreds of millions of adherents of the three great monotheistic religions are intimately associated with its scenes and historical events. Any solution of the Palestine question should take into consideration these religious interests."

If we will but stop to remember we will realize that this bit of land is richer in meaning than any other area of its size in the world. Jerusalem is not alone—almost every foot of the whole of Palestine has religious, historic and archaeological significance. Have we forgotten that this is the Holy Land, dotted with beloved sites sacred to the Christian world—the hills where Jesus preached, the wayside wells where he paused and drank and taught forgiveness, the roads he walked while instructing with parables of charity and humility. Here are the villages where he lodged and accepted all men, even publicans and sinners, as brothers. Here is his birthplace, Bethlehem. Here is his childhood home, Nazareth. Do we Christians not remember? Must we not speak up, remind ourselves that we have a voice in this land, too?

And Palestine has sites equally sacred for the Jews. Bethlehem was also the birthplace of the Psalmist. Under the oak of Mamre Abraham entertained angels unawares. The Israelites drank at the Jerico spring, that city famed in song and story. On Mount Gilboa Saul's sons were slain and he died with them. The ruins of Solomon's buildings still stand at Megiddo. It was at Shechem that Jacob's sons avenged their sister's honor. At Dothan Joseph was sold by his brethren. And it was at the Rock Moriah itself that David saw the angel with the flaming sword and the prophets through succeeding generations thundered their denunciations of evil-doing.

For the Moslem's also, this land is sacred. Abraham, their progenitor as well as the progenitor of the Jews, lies buried in Hebron and Moslems guard that tomb with the greatest care. They believe their Prophet Mohammed ascended to heaven from Jerusalem and they guard that site too.

And there is great history here. Megiddo was the famous battle ground called Armageddon. From Tyre, where the Tyrian purple denoted rank, merchants traded with the Mediterranean world. Magnificent ruins can still be seen at the sites of the Roman coast cities. The Horns of Hattin was the scene of Crusader defeat and the loss of the True Cross. Surely we have not forgotten these religious and historical meanings. Palestine has all these and other sites innumerable and almost equally important.

So let us rescue this Holy Land from the grasping hands of the contentious and accord it the status that is its due. Beneath its scars lies a character of the utmost nobility. Let us treat this sacred spot as a great King, clothe it with fine robes, seat it on a throne, put a crown upon its head that all may do homage.

Let us do this. This land is a monument to God and three great faiths—let us make it a monument. An International Monument, deservedly the first. Let us do this.

The Plan

Name: PALESTINE INTERNATIONAL MONUMENT.

Area: 10,429 square miles.

Reason for Being: There are two reasons that are of paramount importance.

First. To solve the seemingly insoluble problem as it exists at present and put an end to a situation that has grown into a permanent danger to the world.

Second. To set Palestine apart, in a class above world politics and thus give it a special, superior status that will command the respect of world opinion, a respect that may in time grow to such magnitude that it will keep the Holy Land inviolable, safe and at peace by common consent.

Means of Accomplishment: Such an International Monument would have to be set up by a world organization—the United Nations. Should the UN adopt the plan, Palestine will be the *first* International Monument.

To administer it, a new and Specialized Agency of the UN would have to be set up.

If that agency is to achieve its purpose of taking Palestine out of politics it must of necessity be an entirely separate department, unrelated in any way to any of the other Specialized Agencies of the UN and strictly nonpolitical, in the same way that our own National Parks system is unrelated to our Department of State and our school system. The best features of our own and of the park systems of other countries could serve as models.

To guard against domination by any of the Great Powers, none would be represented in the personnel of the Parks Service and certainly no member of the Security Council would be represented. The foresters and trained park personnel would be chosen entirely from small countries, just as the guards at the Vatican are. They might come from such small countries in the Western Hemisphere as Uruguay or Peru in South America or Costa Rica in Central America; small countries in Europe such as Ireland or Denmark; small countries in Asia such as Afghanistan or Burma; small countries in Africa such as Ethiopia or Liberia. They would administer Palestine just as our own National Parks Service administers our national parks.

Palestine's entire area "from Dan to Beersheba" would be locally policed by a picked force of Rangers, also chosen from small countries, dedicated to that duty only, as our own rangers are. The force would be ample but not prohibitively large, for the whole of Palestine is comparable in area to that administered by our National Parks Service *in California alone*, one state out of forty-eight, and this does not include the National Forests in the state—only the parks.

As to danger of aerial attack or invasion from without, Palestine would be under the protection of whatever forces were working with the UN in the eastern Mediterranean area.

Internal red tape need not be insurmountable.

The present residents of Israel and Arab Palestine

would continue to live in their own homes, just as our residents in our own National Forests do. Our United States government, in order to create national monuments, memorials and parks has bought some private properties and granted residential 99-year leases on others. The same could be done in Palestine. Legitimate private businesses could continue on the same basis on which businesses are licensed and operated in our own national parks.

No encroaching on private property would be allowed. Roads and points of special interest open to the public would be exceedingly well guarded and regulated.

Benefits: Whereas political administration is inherently controversial, park administration is inherently peaceful. Sanity and common sense can prevail if this plan can remove Palestine from the realm of world politics. It would end the deadly and stultifying armistice with its paralyzing restrictions and hair-trigger dangers, and would obviate the necessity for a peace treaty, hitherto impossible to achieve, between Jordan and Israel. It would provide the present residents peace and security. It would engender enormous pride in the fact that their territory was the special spot chosen for a new concept in constructive world cooperation. Unhampered, the UN International Monument authorities could carry out public projects of beautification and water supply that would make this poor skeleton land a fertile and profitable garden spot for its inhabitants.

The hill country of Palestine is made up of narrow canyon-like valleys cut down deep between limestone hills. Local water conservation dams spaced in the valleys could irrigate this land and make it grow food ample for its population, both Arabs and Jews.

The Population: Now we come to the main problem. It too can be worked out, perhaps more easily than was anticipated. It can be worked out and justice done to everyone. First of all, of course, the Arab refugees would have to be taken care of. Every one of them should be offered, not one opportunity but a choice of opportunities: (1) to return to his own farm; (2) to go to a new farm; or (3) to receive training that would lead to a job in the Park Department, either in tree planting and forestry employment; or as a guide or in the department of maintenance of the tourist sites. If he chooses to return to his own farm and if that farm is now occupied by an Israeli, then the Israeli could be settled in the new project, or receive the Park job. If the Arab's home has been destroyed by the Israelis in order to make way for a communal settlement on the site, we could not expect the communal settlement to be destroyed. Instead it would be allowed to continue there, but the former Arab owner would be paid, and well paid, for the farm he had lost.

The Cost: The initial cost of this project will not be light. But if it is regarded by the World Bank as an investment and handled in that way, it can be made to pay for itself and show a profit.

Properly set up, the International Monument should become (to put it on a practical basis) a fabulously lucrative business.

Because of the countless sacred sites which cover the country from one end to the other, Palestine is of prime interest to millions of Christians, Moslems and Jews. Thousands and hundreds of thousands of pilgrims will flock there yearly.

And Palestine can qualify equally well as an attraction for the ordinary traveler and tourist who is not particularly interested in the sacred places. The Dead Sea is the lowest spot on the face of the earth. The Mediterranean coast is a Lido. Palestine has desert, mountains, the Sea of Galilee, the River Jordan. Jerusalem is that rare thing, an authentic walled city whose ramparts and gates are kept in good repair, for they function now in crises, just as they did in the time of the ancient Jebusites.

Some of the points of interest run through vast chronological ages and range in character from ancient Canaanite, Egyptian, Hyksos and Philistine relics down through Israelite, Greek, Roman, Christian, Arab, Crusader and Turkish remains. One succeeds the other almost faster than the guide can point out as he drives slowly along—Palestine is so small. Places with tradition and meaning fill the country from its heart to its borders.

Pilgrims and tourists, if given an opportunity, will come in never-ending streams to see these sights. They will stop at local hotels and spend money in the shops for native goods and handcrafts. Every section of the country will benefit because the famous places extend to the farthest corners.

So, even if the initial cost is heavy, the money will be used constructively, to create something that will be self-sustaining and may, and probably will, eventually show a handsome profit.

Who Will Decide: Those who will decide whether to adopt this Plan of a Palestine International Monument, or to reject it and let things remain as they are, will be those immediately concerned: the Arabs and the Israelis, the United Nations members, and the chief creators of Israel, the American-Jews.

As has already been stated, the Arabs may consent to

any plan that provides a dignified way out of their present desperate situation. Almost a million of them are living in refugee camps. Those resident in eastern Palestine are governed, not always satisfactorily, by the Hashemite Kingdom of Jordan, now in the greatest financial straits itself, for it has neither the subsidy nor the military protection it formerly had from Britain.

Israel's situation is equally desperate, perhaps we might say even more desperate, for while Jordan is surrounded by friendly Arab nations who can and will help defend her, Israel is one small nation alone in the hostile world of the Middle East.

She has many internal problems, one of the more serious being that of how to absorb her own new immigrants. Jobs have to be found for them, they have to learn to pay their way, a task not easy in a poor country with few opportunities. It is made still more difficult by the limited abilities of the new immigrants, many of whom came from a primitive way of life and have never seen modern industrial methods. Perhaps they do not speak any of the languages commonly used in Israel which makes their training for any career more difficult. It would seem logical that Israel might welcome a change that would provide many new jobs and an opportunity for increased prosperity for its people.

So long as the situation continues as it is, Israel will doubtless maintain its huge army. That will necessitate an enormous allotment for military purposes from the yearly budget.

But Israel's greatest problem is that she is not self-sustaining, and has never paid her own way.

Most of her financing comes from abroad, specifically from the United States, in loans and gifts from our government and in private gifts from American-Jews. If these foreign funds and contributions were cut off, as they could conceivably be in certain contingencies, the Israeli government could not pay its month-to-month expenditures, to say nothing of paying interest on its government bonds.

Any nation that cannot support itself inevitably faces a hazardous future. Israel's strong talking point is that better times will come when she can come to terms with the Arabs, sit down across the table from them and agree on the economic cooperation that will provide convenient, nearby markets in the great Arab world for the industrial products of the Israeli state.

This is wishful thinking. No Arab government will sit down at the table and talk economic cooperation while three-quarters of a million refugees are forbidden by Israel to return to their homes and while Mr. Ben-Gurion sends military expeditions into neighboring Arab countries to seize and hold Arab territory.

As in any business venture, the man who will really decide the issue is the man who puts up the financial backing—in this case the American-Jew. His will be the deciding voice for he is the man who did more than any other to create Israel. His money, more than any other, has kept Israel going. He has bought Israel bonds as an investment; his gifts, taken out of one pocket, have paid the bond interest put in the other pocket. His wife has raised the money that has built Israel's hospitals and clinics and her present fund raising activities now maintain them.

These—the American-Jews—are the investors who now own a big stake in Israel's future existence. Israel's survival and eventual success is financially important to them. If Israel fails the Jewish-American stockholder loses his money.

No investor wants to wake up and find his bonds worthless—you would not, I would not, and the American-Jew, good businessman that he is, does not want this loss either.

He knows the outlook is not good, that Israel, already over capitalized, is operating at a deficit and as things are now can never liquidate the bonds at par value. So he faces the necessity of deciding whether to throw good money after bad, to give money out of his own pocket so the Israel bonds will not default—or to write the whole thing off as a loss and get out before losing more.

What he has not thought of (and he should have thought of it, for he *is* a good businessman) is a Change in Management, and Refinancing. A business that has reached the point of diminishing returns can sometimes be salvaged by reorganization under a new management and a refinancing that will make a big business out of a little business, add new lines, and find new markets. Under such a reorganization the old Israel bonds held by the stockholders could be exchanged for other, sounder securities, such as bonds for a Jordan Valley Authority which would be a replica of our own TVA, or for Park bonds that would pay themselves out at an excellent rate of interest.

The Decision: We have considered the highlights of the International Monument Plan. Before we decide to adopt it, we must weigh it pro and con. We must judge it by the same rules we have used previously. That is, we must count the points for, and the points against, then give the decision to the side having the majority.

As we have seen, the Park Plan will restore their *hu-*

man rights to the Palestinians. As human beings, the Arab refugees must be given back their place in society—nothing can be solved in Palestine until this basic human right is fulfilled. It *cannot* be fulfilled, the way things are now. Israel cannot take the Arabs back because she has no place for them, and she cannot pay them for their properties because she has no money.

But these refugees are a part of mankind, in this case a test-sample of mankind. The whole struggle upward from savagery to civilization is ultimately to attain one purpose—the betterment of mankind, of people, individuals, of fathers, mothers and children such as these refugees. If their inherent rights are recognized and respected, then the religious and political rights will fall into their proper places.

This inalienable right of the individual is a basic theory of democracy, the groundwork, the foundation on which democracy is built. That foundation must be stable if the edifice is to be sound. That foundation, stone by stone, is built on individuals, each person in his rightful place in the society of men.

This is not just an idealistic theory, but a practical plan for democracy which must be worked out, country by country, area by area, until all the people everywhere in the world are free. Let us try to work it out, this problem of human rights, in one small but vital spot, Palestine.

As for the *religious* rights: The International Monument Plan, if adopted will make equal for the first time in this area the rights of Moslems, Christians and Jews. That is point two in the Plan's favor.

And for *political* rights: The Plan will free part of the population, the Palestinian Arabs, from outside domination, *i.e.*, by the Hashemite Kingdom of Jordan. We can count this as a half-point in our score.

This gives an overwhelming majority of two and one-half out of three, which would seem to indicate that adoption of the plan is infinitely preferable to the *status quo*.

Surely it should not be difficult for the people of the United Nations, Israel, Arab Palestine and Jewish-America to choose this good and constructive plan in preference to the frustration, hate, violence, bloodshed, poverty, indebtedness and uncertainty that now exist. Now the decision should be easy for all concerned—not only to consent, but to take an active part in building this beautiful ideal.

The Result: If we say yes this will be for the world as well as for the Arabs and the Jews an historic "first." For never in the whole long course of civilization have a people been made *citizens of the world.* It will be a momentous event, a part of history, and some day the names on this list of "first citizens of the world" will be pointed to by their descendants with the same intense pride some Americans feel in speaking of their ancestors who came over on the Mayflower.

It will be especially wonderful for the refugees, both Arabs and Jews, a real rags-to-riches miracle when they make the change from a status of displaced, homeless persons to world citizens. It will be the actual fulfillment of the Biblical prophecy that the last shall be first—the most poignant and at the same time the most gratifying "happy ending" ever told in all the annals of literature. Never before and perhaps never again will a million people be metamorphosed from absolute hopelessness to hope and security by one decision. We may be sure the whole world will rejoice with them.

Then this poor "trouble spot" can be changed, too, transformed into something fine and beautiful and inspiring, a great International Monument in which the whole world can take pride, a suitable setting for its heart and center, Jerusalem.

Jerusalem, the city set on a hill where so far as we know God was first worshipped, may then fulfill its manifest destiny and become the loveliest shrine in the world—a real symbol in every way of the true faith, a fitting tribute to God, a light shining, illuminating the dark places of the earth, and once again as when we first knew it, a City of Peace.

NOTES

NOTES

1. *British Government Official Memorandum* to UN Special Committee on Palestine, July, 1947: "When the first census was taken in 1922 the Jewish community, already growing as a result of immigration, then numbered 84,000."

2. *Israeli Ministry of Foreign Affairs Memorandum* to the Technical Committee of the Palestine Conciliation Commission, July 28, 1949: "The individual return of Arab Refugees to their former places of residence is an impossible thing."

Israeli Ordinances expropriating Arab property:

(1) The Abandoned Area Ordinance, 1948
(2) Emergency Regulations, 1948 (Cultivation of Waste Lands)
(3) The Absentee Property Regulations, 1948
(4) The Absentee Property Law, 1956
(5) The Land Acquisition Law, 1956

3. Sir John Bagot Glubb, "Glubb Tells How Our Mid-East Enemies Work," *Life*, April 16, 1956: "When the Israelis captured Lydda a pathetic crowd of men, women and children fled from the town across the fields with only the clothes they stood up in. It was a blazing day in the coastal plain and the fugitives had no water. I remember the next day seeing one tragic woman crouching exhausted with two children beside the road. Yesterday she had had four children but the two youngest had died in their tracks of thirst in that terrible flight. No one who saw that heart-breaking exodus—the haggard women, the exhausted children, the anguish, the panic, the tears—no one who saw it will forget it for the rest of his life."

4. *Border Incidents,* Major Vagn Benneke, former head of the UN Truce Supervision Organization.

5. *Time,* April 2, 1956: "Glubb Pasha, trusted and devoted servant of old King Abdullah, kept the Israeli border quiet. . . . General Glubb patiently took him [young King Hussein] on a tour of the 350-mile Israeli frontier to show him how much the Legion's 20,000 men had to defend against Israeli's 250,000-man army."

Don Cook, "Tough Little Army," *Saturday Evening Post,* February 18, 1956: "They not only can rush 250,000 men and women into uniforms within forty-eight hours. They can also mobilize every bus, taxicab, truck and private automobile in the country into army motor pools."

6. *Report, Mixed Armistice Commission,* October 15, 1953: "The crossing of the demarcation line by a force approximating one-half of a battalion from the Israeli regular army, fully equipped, into Qibya village on the night of 14–15 October, 1953, to attack the inhabitants by firing from automatic weapons and throwing grenades and using bangalore torpedoes together with TNT explosive, by which forty-one dwelling houses and a school building were completely blown up, resulting in the cold-blooded murder of forty-two lives, including men, women (and) children, and the wounding of fifteen persons and the damage of a police car, (and) at the same time the crossing of a part of the same group into Shuqba village (are) a breach of article III, paragraph 2 of the General Armistice Agreement."

7. *Report, Mixed Armistice Commission,* April 30, 1954: "The Mixed Armistice Commission condemns Israel in the strongest terms for this latest aggression."

8. *Resolution of Censure,* Mixed Armistice Commission, September 3, 1954.

9. *Egypt-Israel Mixed Armistice Commission,* March 6, 1955: This was "a prearranged and planned attack ordered by Israeli authorities . . . committed by Israeli regular army forces."

This action condemned by Security Council, March 29, 1955, *Resolution* S/3378.

10. *UN Document* S/3430 (par. 16). Statement by Chief of Staff, UN Truce Supervision Organization: "An Israeli light armored unit, in half-tracks, penetrated into *Egyptian-controlled territory* and advanced to the police station at Khan Yunis, taking it under machine gun fire and subsequently destroying it by heavy explosive charges."

11. *New York Times*, Nov. 3, 1955: United Nations officials "expressed grave concern to the permanent representative of Israel at the *military action by the Israeli army*."

12. *UN Document* S/3516, par. 1 to 10.

13. *UN Document* S/3685.

14. W. F. T. Castle, *Syrian Pageant*, p. 153: "Sinai, an integral part of the kingdom of Egypt (as it has nearly always been throughout history)."

15. *UN Document* S/PV635, p. 41.

16. Wm. Langer, *An Encyclopedia of History*, section on Early Empires:

Crete. "c. 4000-B.C. The Bronze Age in Crete" (p. 46).

Canaan. "3200-2100, Early Bronze Age" (p. 29).

Greece. "3000-200 B.C. The Greeks, speaking a language belonging to the western division of the Indo-European family, began to spread southward from the northwestern corner of the Balkans" (p. 47).

Egypt. "c. 2900-2700 B.C. Dynasties I-II (capital, Thinis)" (p. 23).

Assyria. "c. 2600-2000 B.C. The city of Asshur, at first Sumerian" (p. 27).

Babylonia. "c. 1900-1600 B.C. The first Dynasty of Babylon" (p. 26).

Mitanni. "1580-1350 B.C. . . . Carchemish . . . and Aleppo remained under the rule of Mitanni." "—outside pressure (Hittites and Amorites in the north)" (p. 23).

17. W. F. Albright, *Archaeology of Palestine*, pp. 55-57: "The Carmel individuals proved to represent a mixed race,

intermediate between palaeanthropic man *(Homo neanderthalensis)* and neanthropic man *(Homo sapiens)* and reflecting several stages between. . . . It would appear that *Homo sapiens* came from the southeast into Europe, driving *Neanderthaloid* man before him, and interbreeding with the conquered at the same time."

18. *Ibid.*, p. 57.

19. *Ibid.*, pp. 60-61: "typical early Mediterraneans, with slender bony structure, long-headed (dolichocephalic) and delicate features; the men averaged only a little over 5 feet in height. Since very similar human skeletons have been found in the Badarian of Egypt as well as in late chalcolithic Gezer and Byblus, it seems to follow that these folk belonged to the ancestral *Semito-Hamitic stock*, which had not yet become so sharply differentiated into linguistic and national groups as later."

20. *Ibid.*, p. 62.

21. *Ibid.*, p. 65.

22. *Ibid.*, p. 74: "During the latter part of this period, Palestine and Phoenicia were exposed to strong Egyptian influence and the powerful kings of the Thinite period *seem to have extended their empire* into Asia.

23. *Ibid.*, p. 85: "Monuments attesting to direct connections with the Egyptian Court as far back as the early nineteenth century B.C., have been found far north at Ugarit and far east at Qatna, northeast of Hums. . . . The Execration Tests even enable us to draw the boundary of the direct sphere of *Egyptian control* across central Syria north of Damascus to the Eleutherus Valley in central Phoenicia."

24. Harry M. Orlinsky, *Ancient Israel*, p. 18: "There appears to be good reason for associating the Biblical Hebrews with some of these far-flung Habiru. . . . Hebrew origins begin essentially with Abraham the son of Terah (Genesis 11), whose origin is located in the region of Ur in southern Mesopotamia, less than thirty miles from Larsa, where Habiru were found about 1900 B.C." "—And after Terah died Abra-

ham took his own immediate family and began the long journey to Canaan."

25. Langer, *op. cit.*, p. 23: "Egypt . . . Foreign domination, (Dynasties XV-XVI) (Hyksos), 1680-1580."

26. Small ivory statue, "Hyksos king, (possibly King Khayan)," Fig. 178, No. 54678, Fifth Egyptian Room, Case F. British Museum, London.

27. Langer, *op. cit.*, p. 23: "The great Thutmosis III (1501-1447) in 19 years (17 campaigns) conquered Palestine (through the victory of Megiddo in 1479)."

28. V. Gordon Childe, *What Happened in History*, p. 78: "All the practical science of the ancient smiths and miners was certainly embedded in an unpractical matrix of magic ritual. Assyrian texts, even in the First Millenium B.C., contain hints of what such rituals involved—foetuses and virgin's blood."

29. W. F. Albright, *The Biblical Period*, p. 18: "—the period of Egyptian decline which followed the death of Marniptah about 1225 B.C. For a decade three weak rulers held the facade of empire together, but the Egyptian dependencies, extremely restive under Marniptah, must have broken away almost entirely from their allegiance to the Pharaoh. After this decade, Egypt fell into complete anarchy for nearly a generation, as vividly portrayed in the preamble to the famous Papyrus Harris."

30. Harold Peake and Herbert John Fleure, *The Horse and the Sword*, pp. 2-3: "After 1200 B.C., an important crisis occurred throughout the greater part of the Old World. In 1169 B.C. the Kassite Dynasty suddenly came to an end. . . . About 1205 the death of Merneptah II was accompanied by the fall of the 19th Dynasty in Egypt. . . . About 1200 B.C. the Hittite documents suddenly cease. . . . In 1194 Troy was destroyed by the Achaeans. . . . After these crises we witness the rise of the Greeks, the Phoenicians, the Philistines, the Hebrews." *Cambridge Ancient History* (Macmillan, 1926), Vol. II, p. 472: "The end of the Bronze Age in the 12th cen-

tury saw the coming of the Iron Age, the fall of ruling powers and the decline of Civilization. . . . Everything appears to have lost its stability, and confusion and invasion to have precluded any return to peace."

31. Langer, *op. cit.*, p. 24: "Merneptah (1225-1215) under whom, probably, Moses led the Israelites out of Egypt."

The theory of the date of 1224 B.C. for the Exodus is considered probable by many historians. Their line of reasoning is as follows: Ramesses II the Great must have been the Pharaoh of the Oppression for throughout his unusually long reign of 67 years he was the most monumental builder in that period of Egyptian history. The Bible states that the Israelites actually built a store city of his name. (Exod., 1:11) At his death in 1225 B.C. he was succeeded by his aging and ineffective son Merneptah. Immediately Moses, the Israelite fugitive in Midian, dared return. He spent some months in cowing Pharaoh by means of the plagues and in raising the Israelites, so that their Exodus occurred in the following year, 1224 B.C. If this is true and if the period of their wandering in the desert was 40 years, then that would place the date of their entry into Canaan as 1184 B.C.

32. Some authorities believe this crown was of pleated leather. Whatever it was, we may be sure it was not leather. Leather, when wet, becomes limp and will not stand up but lops over. When it dries it curls and warps—any Philistine with that kind of headdress would have excited the utmost derision. Feathers, on the other hand, will stand up when wet for they have a spine and will resume their normal form when dried. They are practically weightless, protect the head from the sun and what is more important are so constructed that when standing in a crown they will deflect a light missile upward and backward as our American Indians well knew when they chose feathers for their war bonnets.

33. W. F. Albright, *Recent Discoveries in Bible Lands,* p. 90, gives the date 1175-1154 B.C. for the reign of Ramesses III. (The chronology of this particular period of ancient his-

tory is under almost constant revision as new archaeological evidence comes to light.)

34. Albright Chronology, *Recent Discoveries in Bible Lands* (loose leaf).

35. I Chron., 29: 27.

36. II Chron., 9: 30.

37. Wm. Langer, *op. cit.,* p. 31: "586-538 B.C. The Jews under Babylonian rule."

38. Albright Chronology: "538-330 B.C. The Jews under Persian rule."

39. Albright Chronology.

40. Funk & Wagnalls *Dictionary:* "chlamys (klemus) *Greek Antiquity,* A short cloak caught up on the shoulder, worn by hunters, soldiers and horsemen."

41. Castle, *op. cit.,* p. 52.

42. *Ibid.,* p. 54: "By 70 B.C. he [Tigranes the Armenian king] was ruler over an empire extending from Ararat to Sinai."

43. Albright Chronology.

44. Langer, *op. cit.,* p. 111: "The suppression of the revolt all but depopulated Judea."

45. *Ibid.,* p. 32: "63 B.C.-A.D. 395, Palestine under Roman rule" (from Rome). P. 120: "A.D. 395, Jan. 17. Theodosius died at Milan. The Roman Empire was divided between his elder son Arcadius, made Augustus in the east, and the younger son Honorius, made Augustus in the west."

From that time on, the Eastern Roman Empire, whose capital was Constantinople (Byzantium), ruled Palestine until that territory was lost to Persia in A.D. 614. Roman rule ended in Palestine with Persian conquest: Antioch, Apameia, Emesa, Kaisareia; Damascus (613), Jerusalem (614), Egypt (619).

46. *Ibid.,* p. 127: "A.D. 628-629 Kobad II [Persia] who made peace with Heraclius (Eastern Roman Empire) on the basis of an exchange of *conquests* and prisoners."

47. *Ibid.,* pp. 184-5: "A.D. 634-641. The Arab Conquests.

Damascus (635); the Battle of Yarmuk (636) gained all Syria; capitulation of Jerusalem (638). The seacoast occupied."

48. Arnold J. Toynbee, *A Study of History*, p. 17: "The cataclysmic conquests of the primitive Muslim Arabs seem to respond antistrophically in the rhythm of history, to the cataclysmic conquests of Alexander. Like these, they changed the face of the world in half a dozen years."

Castle, *op. cit.*, p. 90: "Arabisation . . . had two aspects—linguistic, by which the population of the conquered countries acquired Arabic as their mother tongue, and racial, by which masses of pure Arab immigrants settled and intermarried with the Syrian population. Palestine and Trans-jordan received the largest proportion."

49. Langer, *op. cit.*, p. 186: "The Omayyad Caliphate, 661-750. . . . Damascus." P. 188: "The Abbasid Capiphate, 750-1100. . . . Baghdad." P. 262: "968-1171. The Fatimid Dynasty. . . . Egypt."

50. Castle, *op. cit.*, p. 92.

51. Langer, *op. cit.*, p. 254f. A. J. Toynbee, *op. cit.*, p. 28: "—the invasions of the Saljuq Turks which provoked the crusading counter-attack on our Western society."

52. Castle, *op. cit.*, p. 94.

53. Langer, *op. cit.*, p. 256.

54. Castle, *op. cit.*, p. 105.

55. *Ibid.*, p. 107.

56. Langer, *op. cit.*, p. 258.